ARKANA

ABSOLUTE LIVING

The late Karlfried Graf Dürckheim was acclaimed throughout Europe as the leading reconciler of Oriental and Western thought, as reflected in his numerous books. His best-known works are *The Way of Transformation: Daily Life as Spiritual Exercise*, *The Call for the Master*, *Zen and Us*, *The Japanese Cult of Tranquillity*, *Hara: The Vital Centre of Man*, and *The Grace of Zen*.

Born into the Bavarian nobility, he survived four years at the front in World War I and was saved at the last minute from a Spartacist firing squad during the abortive Bavarian Revolution of 1919. He later gave up his inheritance to undergo spiritual training as a psychologist and philosopher. Influenced by his association with Klee, Kandinsky, and Mies van der Rohe, his initiation into an esoteric group in Munich, and his studies with Heidegger, D. T. Suzuki, and others, he spent the Nazi years in Japan and went on to found the world-famous Center for Initiatory Psychotherapy in the Black Forest after World War II.

ABSOLUTE LIVING

THE OTHERWORLDLY
IN THE WORLD AND
THE PATH TO
MATURITY

KARLFRIED GRAF DÜRCKHEIM

TRANSLATED BY
VINCENT NASH

ARKANA

ARKANA BOOKS
Published by the Penguin Group
Viking Penguin, a division of Penguin Books USA Inc.,
375 Hudson Street, New York, New York 10014, U.S.A.
Penguin Books Ltd, 27 Wrights Lane, London W8 5TZ, England
Penguin Books Australia Ltd, Ringwood, Victoria, Australia
Penguin Books Canada Ltd, 10 Alcorn Avenue, Suite 300,
Toronto, Ontario, Canada M4V 3B2
Penguin Books (N.Z.) Ltd, 182–190 Wairau Road,
Auckland 10, New Zealand

Penguin Books Ltd, Registered Offices:
Harmondsworth, Middlesex, England

First published in Arkana Books 1992

1 3 5 7 9 10 8 6 4 2

Originally published in Switzerland as *Überweltliches Leben in der Welt*
by Otto Wilhelm Barth Verlag, a division of Scherz Verlag, Bern und Munchen.
© 1968 by Otto Wilhelm Barth Verlag Weilheim/Obb.

LIBRARY OF CONGRESS CATALOGING IN PUBLICATION DATA
Dürckheim, Karlfried, Graf, 1896–
[Überweltliches Leben in der Welt. English]
Absolute living: the otherworldly in the world and the path to
maturity / Karlfried Graf Dürckheim ; translated by Vincent Nash.
p. cm.
Translation of: Überweltliches Leben in der Welt.
Includes bibliographical references.
ISBN 0 14 01.9452 5
1. Life. 2. Supernatural. I. Title.
BD431.D8713 1992
128—dc20   91-30123

Printed in the United States of America
Set in Palatino
Designed by Brian Mulligan

FOR MARIA HIPPIUS

PREFACE

THE WRONG DISTINCTIONS—AND THE RIGHT ONE

Today, as always, the old is pitting its sluggish weight against the new. It is only where the light of otherworldly Life is dawning in the world that the mists in which a one-sided ignorance of Being has shrouded the truth of existence are dispersing. At those points, the antitheses generated by an immature and limited vision are revealed as false distinctions, and the way clears to the only distinction that makes sense: that between witnesses to Life, who are willing to sacrifice themselves utterly to serve it, and prisoners of the ego, who have made themselves the tools of the malevolent or even well-intentioned powers that distort or stand in the way of absolute Life, that is, Life from Being.

Why are the young rebelling today? What is the conflict all about? To see it as a battle between good and evil is a crude oversimplification. Behind those antitheses there lies something totally different, something that really gives the terms "for" and "against" a meaning: Life.

Whenever organic, tradition-hallowed communities become soulless organizational units, their members are thrown back upon themselves and, all too often, the encounter with their own inner core shows them that the authorities that rule their lives are hollow and unconvincing.

Champions of order can be enemies of Life, and enemies of order can be witnesses to Life. Today, we are seeing a widespread rebellion against the champions of an order that has become inimical to Life because it blocks all change. But we are surrounded, too, by powers that threaten Life by rejecting form entirely.

The essence of Life is form *and* change, permeable form and formed permeability; absence of form and stagnation of form are equally effective in making it impossible. We are right to reject order when Life inspires us to do so. But we are wrong to make revolution a pretext for declaring war on every order. The enemy of Life threatens or destroys it in two ways: by dissipating it and by paralyzing it. In both cases, Life slows to a stop.

The movement toward perfection of form and the converse movement that brings perfected form home to the All-One together make up the eternal rhythm of Life. Whenever the poles turn into antitheses, false distinctions are created; this is what happens when the dialectical movement in which Life reveals its vital essence hardens into fixed positions. One result of this is the kind of futile argument that is all too frequent between adherents of the Eastern and Western traditions.

The conflict between "East" and "West" often makes hardened opponents of people whose outlook has a male and patriarchal coloring, and people whose values are basically female and matriarchal. But just as the male and female elements are an essential part of every human being, so they are essential to the well-being of the whole community—in both East and West. The distinctions that arise in this way are false distinctions, and their sterility is clearest in religious conflict.

Religions divide; true religious feeling unites, for it is rooted in a primal experience that all humans share, and follows the rhythm of a dialectical movement between belief in a Godhead remote from humankind and mystical experience of an All-in-One that cancels all dualities. Conditional and yet fruitful, the emphasis in this movement lies first on one side, then on the other. Division only sets in when one of the two positions becomes the fixed and final aim of a religion. In fact, it is only in the to-and-fro movement between them that the otherworldly reveals itself as Life in the religious sphere. The time has now come to forget the false distinctions born of the difference between the Eastern and the Western spirits and to look at the real distinctions. Once we do this, there runs, clear through all the differences between East and West, the division between the deathly stasis of clung-to positions and the dynamic movement of true religious life, manifesting itself in polar oscillation and repeatedly carrying the fixities of objective belief home into the experience of supra-objective Life.

When *Being* becomes experience, another increasingly common and sterile distinction can also be left behind: the distinction between those who believe in God—Christians and other non-Christian believers—and all those who do not, Marxists and humanists, but also Buddhists and others. It is true that believers and "unbelievers" have recently started to talk, and this certainly marks an improvement on the old, radical intolerance. But whether they fight or smile (not always honestly) and agree to differ, whether they laugh at or pity one another, their opposition breeds false distinctions. It is precisely the "peaceful" juxtaposition of the two parties that conceals a distinction that is vital, and particularly so today: the distinction between those who have no contact with the Absolute, and want none, and those who are vitally connected to it—not simply because their belief is intact, but also because they truly experience it, or have a fundamental openness of spirit that gives them an instinctive respect for the numinous and holy, and makes them receptive to it.

There are people who believe in God, who eagerly profess a religion, and yet have no contact whatsoever with Being, let alone the experience of Being that remakes and transforms. There are also people who no longer know, or want to know, anything about God or Christ, and yet are in genuine contact with the Absolute. They show this in the transparency of what they are, in their selfless, courageous, and unreserved commitments, in their brave endurance of hardship and, even as scientists and technicians, in the numinous inspiration that underlies everything they do and gives it an invincible strength. And so the dividing line between those who are touched by the Absolute and those who are deaf to its call runs straight through the false distinction between believers and nonbelievers. Often enough, feeling for otherworldly Life and its manifestation in the world is stifled when the champions of dogmatic, institutional creeds write off the personal experience of Being as merely natural, or side unexpectedly with the rationalists and dismiss it as merely subjective.

A similar distinction manifests itself in the nonreligious sphere in the antithesis between spiritualists and materialists, and also between those who look out and find their satisfaction in molding the world to serve their own security and pleasures, and those who look in, seek the path to maturity, and travel it. But just as the truth of Life knows nothing of the division between matter and spirit, and vanishes whenever either claims to be the whole, so working in the world and inner maturing belong indissolubly together. This is why people who say that attending to the soul reduces our worldly efficiency, or that the world prevents us from traveling the road that leads inward, are again making false distinctions.

Our worldly skills and the value of what we do in the

world increase as we mature, and the only way of maturing genuinely is to take the world head-on, and face up to its demands. Inner and outer world are transcended, however, by the Absolute's claim to express itself in both—in its own language. Like soul and body, the inner and the outer world are two sides of a living whole, in which the individual lives himself or herself out as a person. It is not the inner and the outer world that make the difference between human beings —but the presence of the Absolute. Human beings are divided into the mature and the immature, into those who have a responsible knowledge of the Absolute and try to conform to it and those who do not. They are divided into those who accept the demands of practice and those who do not, and what finally counts is whether they try to realize themselves in a humanity that relies on *immanent transcendence* to lift humanness to a higher level, and so fulfill their true human destiny.

CONTENTS

WHAT IT ALL LEADS TO

ABSOLUTE LIVING

THE GOAL

MATURITY

What matters today is changing human beings in a way that frees them from the prison of static, world-bound thinking into a dynamic process in which they *mature*, overcome outside obstacles, grow beyond inner barriers, and enter on the way of true self-fulfillment, self-fulfillment that links them with otherworldly Life. What matters is people who unite with their true nature and find higher freedom as *persons*.

"Personal maturity" is not simply a matter of knowing and being able to do certain things, and not just a question of ethical stability. It means being remade by the Absolute. People who are mature in this sense do not have more than others and cannot do more than others, but *are* more than people who have not attained maturity. The kind of maturity we mean leaves them free, not simply to make their own decisions on worldly matters, but also to witness to their own true nature, and to the transcendent order woven into it. They can not only do what they want (because maturity makes them want the licit only), but can *be* what they fundamentally are—what God and their own true nature make them, what they themselves aspire to be and what they are meant to be. This being permitted to be what one really is—a real human being and the very specific human being that one's own true nature intends and destines one to be—is the central issue of our age.

In its nature, origins, and remedies, the plight of the neurotic has significant similarities to and connections with the general plight of human beings today. Therapists are confronted not only with the most extreme cases, but also with those that best represent the malady typical of the present age: the inability, in spite of all one has, knows, or can do, to be the person one basically is. The reasons for this are very like those that therapists find when they trace neurosis back to childhood. The most common are: the crushing of children's independence, which demoralizes and paralyzes them; lack of insight, which prevents them from genuinely connecting with their own inner selves; and the withholding of love, which throws them back upon themselves. These are the factors that surface later in anxiety, guilt, and contact neuroses. They have clear parallels in certain features typical of modern life; thus individual freedom is much vaunted, but the individual's real scope for independent self-assertion is increasingly restricted and eroded, and his or her individuality ignored. Indeed, men and women today have almost entirely lost the feeling of being accepted and addressed, let alone valued and cherished, for what they really are. Like children, they are adjusting in ways that make them feel safer, help them to get through, and minimize the pain of living in a world that contradicts their true nature. But the more these adjustments take root and become second nature, the greater the barriers they place in the way of self-realization, since they act like neurosis in sealing off true nature. Whenever the anguish caused by this choking of the self builds to a point where it borders on the unbearable, the individual is ready to take a leap that bursts the chains and throws open the door to something totally new.

Our age is reducing people increasingly to impotence, but it is also doing more than any age before it to wake their feeling for inner freedom. It may rob them of maturity and confine them in godless systems, but it also transforms them through suffering and brings them to the threshold of the inner experiences that generate maturity. Attaining maturity marks a turning point in human development. The new element is the self-reliance of the individual whose transcendent true nature allows him or her to find the way to *otherworldly Life*.

Maturing in this way marks a decisive—perhaps we should say *the* decisive—third step in the three-stage process of personal development, a basic pattern that is already clear in the three successive phases of human life: childhood, emergence of the adult personality in the juxtaposition of ego and world, and the maturity of old age. The process here is one in which wholeness is followed by diversification—diversification that threatens dissolution but, if all goes well, comes back to wholeness on a higher plane. The initial form (childhood) is a living whole, in which inner and outer, heaven and earth, ego and world are still interwoven and combined. The poles then separate, and self-consciousness develops in the antitheses of inner and outer, ego and world, instinct and intellect, conditional and unconditional, becoming and ceasing to be, and so on. As this ego-object consciousness develops, life's original wholeness is broken, and we assert ourselves as what we are and in opposition to the world. As we swing between the ego's claims and the world's demands, we are constantly in danger of becoming alienated from our own true nature, of losing ourselves to the world and being devoured by it. If we succeed in making the transition into old age successfully, however, the third stage offers us the chance of recovering wholeness on a higher level. It is only by taking the detour through alienation from the ground that sustains us that we can one day find ourselves in what we really are, that is, in Being that embraces and resolves all the contradictions of being-in-the-world. It is at this point that we must link back to the Absolute within us and so satisfy the one essential condition for fulfillment of our human destiny. This choice, between ignoring and heeding the call from the depths of true nature to a new and better way, is being offered to individuals all the time, and it typifies the situation of a whole generation today, as the modern era, which started when the Middle Ages ended, prepares to make way for a new one.

The decisive change that the modern era wrought in humanity's feeling for the self, for the world, and for life was rooted in the individual's emergence from a wholeness that was ultimately sensed religiously into the openness of unlimited life. The implications of this were, and are, twofold: people stop believing that they can understand, control, and order the world with God's help and for God's sake, and start believing that they can do these things unaided and for their own sake. This—the waking of the individual as a scrutinizing, comparing, and reasoning subject, who observes and masters the world objectively—marks a massive step forward in the development of the human spirit. At this point, the rational spirit emerges fully for the first time. It is a mistake to judge that spirit, as so many people do today, solely by its negative effects and condemn it accordingly.

But this development also involves separation from the sustaining ground and sheltering powers of existence, and this spells danger. The danger becomes fatal when the subject, from being firmly anchored in the whole, turns into the overbearing ego, loses contact with the Absolute, and accepts as real only the things that the rationally inquiring spirit can master. When this happens, human self-consciousness also shrinks down into the ego-point in which rational consciousness is rooted—rational consciousness that cuts people off from the transcendent true nature that destines them for personhood. This means loss, and indeed betrayal, of the innermost reality, the reality that encloses them and that reason can no longer grasp. The price of betrayal is a bitter one for, once they have lost contact with their roots, the world in which they operate and which they explain in merely rational terms follows *its own law*. They start by believing that emergence from the old, hallowed order means freedom and independence, but ultimately find themselves the prisoners of the very means they devised for their escape. They start by believing that their own strength can make them free, and that they can force nature to obey them, but ultimately find themselves at the mercy of a massive, self-governing mechanism, which reduces them to minor, impersonal cogs in a vast mechanical process. The more they play the world's game, in an effort to dominate and avoid being crushed by it, the more they themselves become "parts" of it and alienated from their true humanity.

What is the anguish that people today are experiencing as "the heirs of the modern era" and where does it come from? The decisive element is this: the axis on which the whole of life turns is no longer divine Being, unconsciously determining or consciously acknowledged as inner presence, but the individual himself! It is no longer otherworldly Being, but the world, that rules humanity. The center and source of meaning is no longer God, but the human individual, relying on his own rationality, and fancying himself independent and the master of both himself and "his" world! This, however, is a vision in which the whole of life is *secularized*—in which our feeling for existence becomes worldly and we lose our deep roots in transcendence.

When we secularize worldly life, reduce it to something that can be known and organized rationally, and make it the center of our whole existence, we inevitably end by *functionalizing* it too. We ourselves become functionaries—the mere repositories of functions and performances that can be rationally grasped, measured, and assessed.

When people are reduced to productive and functional components of a world that is rationally organized from top to bottom, they effectively cease to exist as individual, personal subjects. *Depersonalization* in this sense goes beyond the "suspension" of the purely individual element and private ego that any community needs, and also beyond the selfless performance that any organized community requires. As the purely secular outlook spreads, "personal" reality, which reason cannot grasp, almost ceases to be taken seriously and is virtually eliminated; for only the things we take seriously are real in our human world. Getting rid of the personal element also means, however, ignoring the mystery of individuality and denying the transcendent depths, that is, the individual's existential wholeness and mode of being.

One of the specific ways in which we can miss human wholeness is by overemphasizing the *male*, active, determining, ordering, and shaping functions of the human spirit, at the expense of the receptive, loosening, liberating *female* energies, which sustain, protect, and transform in secret. This involves an enormous narrowing of focus: the view taken by the objectively determining ego reduces "Logos" to reason and the cosmic forces to "urges."

What really matters here is that our own absolute core—our true nature—is being denied and prevented from manifesting itself in the world. This *true nature* cannot be objectively grasped, but we basically exist from it, are destined to manifest it, and depend on its indwelling presence for the whole maturing process. Today it has been largely sacrificed to the world-*ego*; for reason determines our modern view of reality, and reason is increasingly dismissing anything it cannot grasp—in other words, the "Absolute"—as unreal.

We cannot be truly mature, any more than we can be truly free and independent, until we acknowledge our true nature (otherworldly Life individually present in the worldly body), bring it to consciousness, and merge with it consciously. This is why it is precisely when we fancy that we can ignore true nature, and when we rely on a conception of reality that leaves no room for the Absolute, that we are least mature, least free, and least liberated. Inevitably, we increasingly fall prey to the anguish in which the suppression of true nature expresses itself.

How can we overcome the anguish caused by functionalization and depersonalization? Broadly, we have two options here: we can ignore the demands of true nature and concentrate on working toward superficial harmony; or, as this becomes progressively harder and we start to recognize the root cause of our suffering, we can look for a way that effects inner change and so opens the path to the right kind of outer development as well. However, most people first try to escape by "improving" and building on their old position. *Easy* living is now accepted so unquestioningly as the supreme ideal that any means of bringing it closer seems justified at once. Without thinking, people today sacrifice the inner truth of existence to the doubtful joys of a life without cares. Pain, of course, is something we naturally try to avoid, but whenever it tells us that an inner change is needed, we violate our inner law by attempting to suppress it. Here, however, much of our so-called civilization alarmingly resembles a huge pharmaceutical plant, endlessly churning out new remedies to take all the pain out of endlessly making the same old mistakes.

All the outlooks and attitudes that obstruct the change demanded by our true nature express the same basic urge to reach and hold a position where, without changing ourselves, we can force life to yield us a maximum of tranquillity, pleasure, and enjoyment. Just as the rational ego always basically aims, in theory and in practice, at the fixed and final, so this static tendency always appears when the only thing that counts is life without suffering. Imprisoned in the world-ego, people are ready for anything—except change. Like householders who badly need new quarters but will do anything to stay in the home they know, rather than face the effort of building a new one, people today—unknowingly, but sometimes knowingly and stifling their conscience—use every trick in the book to stay painlessly the way they are. The most common ways of doing this are *conforming, systematically letting go,* or *tuning out on drink or drugs.*

Once people see freedom from suffering as life's only target, they accept the status quo with terrifying complacency, and back away from conflict simply to preserve it. But whenever they do this at the expense of inner truth and whenever their search for superficial, short-term harmony stifles the claims of absolute conscience, the long-term results are bound to be disastrous. So, too, are the long-term results of any "therapy" that aims merely at leaving the patient "well-adjusted" and restoring his or her ability to "function" in a worldly sense.

Conformism is one of the methods that the skilled operator uses to achieve surface harmony and carry on living a life from which anxiety, God, and all thoughts of change have been banished, but there is another magic formula today: *relaxation!* This may seem a natural response to the pressures that necessarily make people tense, but many of the things that are taught and done in the name of "relaxation" are found, on closer inspection, to be centered instead on systematic *dissolution.* Their covert purpose is to allow people to stay the way they are. The techniques that "relax" them quickly also allow them to tense again afterward without asking themselves too many awkward questions; for they actually prevent attitudes that are fundamentally wrong from producing their usual negative effects on the body. The right kind of relaxation aims, however, at the right kind of tension, and not at a mere letting go. Tension and relaxation in this sense are twin aspects of a living whole, and belong together like breathing in and breathing out. Tension and relaxation in the other sense are states that succeed, cause, and exclude each other, and have disastrous effects. *Drink and drugs*, too, are an understandable temptation when we feel torn and divided, since they pull things together—but all they really do is dissolve our tensions in a pleasant blur, without changing anything, and this makes them ultimately unhelpful.

The way to maturity and the way to freedom are the same; putting it more accurately, *true maturity* begins when we take the third step on the path to freedom, which is realized stage-by-stage in our human lives, as divine Life comes progressively to consciousness in us.

This otherworldly Life is the ruling principle in us and in everything else, and it manifests itself in three ways: as inexhaustible *fullness*, as indwelling form, order, and *regularity*, and as all-embracing *unity*. Its fullness makes us affirm existence, its indwelling form gives us the urge to achieve valid form as vessels for the Absolute, and its unity inspires us with a longing to be wholly at one with ourselves, with the world, and with God. These three modes in which Life enters our consciousness are paralleled by three stages in our human struggle to be free. At each of them, Being is present *in* its threefold unity—but it is always present in the language of that stage, and one of its aspects has, as it were, the "upper hand."

Freedom at the first stage expresses itself in an overwhelming love of life, an irresistible urge to experience everything it has to offer. What trying to be free essentially means here is trying to secure a life of throbbing sensuous enjoyment, to combine maximum security with maximum pleasure, happiness, and comfort. There is nothing unnatural in this. Indeed, psychotherapists know that the rigidities we call "neuroses" can often be dissolved only by helping patients to find a way back to free enjoyment of the senses. The urge to enjoy life is a natural human urge, and leaving out the senses shows that something has distorted our primal true nature. But a part must never usurp the functions of the whole, and the senses become dangerous once they start to take over.

Freedom means something utterly different at the second stage, when Life's order, regularity, and aspiration toward perfect form come to consciousness, giving us an instinctive feeling for the "rightness" or "wrongness" of things around us. This is when our own and the world's absurdity and imperfection become a source of anguish, and we feel the inner need for an existence that is not just secure, but meaningful, and the urge toward perfection. We satisfy this urge by serving an idea, a cause, a project—something outside of and bigger than ourselves—and our joy in doing so makes us overlook our own selfish desires, forget who we are, and deny our "puny egos." True nature intends us to achieve *valid form*, and it is valid form that we are secretly seeking and circling, at its bidding, both in ourselves and in everything around us. It is the archetypal form imprinted in our true nature that makes us see the world as a question in need of an answer, as unfinished business that we must complete and perfect. This primal imprint means that "form" is a fundamental aspect of our living, and this is why we respond to it deeply in ourselves and others, and have a very special feeling for the "rightness" and "wrongness" of the world around us ("our" world). Striving for formal perfection, we experience freedom as the legitimate expression of Being's vital, indwelling presence in our true nature, and this allows us to leave ego-nature behind and give ourselves wholly to a cause or community. This capacity for commitment raises us above the limitations of merely conditional existence.

By sharing in the Absolute and serving it, by committing ourselves to an absolute ideal, we develop that *spiritual* freedom that is specifically human. Its finest exponents have always been those men and women who have served certain *values* unconditionally, and have died for their sake—indeed it is sustaining and shielding values that has lent their lives dignity and meaning. The most important of such values is *honor*—honor that we lose by failing to defend the values entrusted to us. An age that has no time for "honor" is a decadent age.

When we say that serving values or a cause makes us free, we mean that the unconditional nature of that service gives us power over ourselves and releases us from our normal human limitations. Achievement replaces pleasure as the source of joy. The finite, sensuous pleasures that echoed Being's fullness are no longer our guiding principle. This role now passes to the absolute demands (absolute because valid under all conditions) of Being's indwelling order and presence, as reflected in valid form. Our freedom here is the freedom that comes of automatically obeying the absolute demands of the conscience that concerns itself with values and with form.

For a long time it seemed that the highest form of freedom was this—the freedom that allowed men and women to serve the Absolute truly, conquer the world's limitations, effectively mediate an objective ideal, and establish themselves as solid "personalities" in the process. This is the freedom that first reveals our spiritual nature and turns us into personalities, but today we are forced to admit that it is still not the freedom that opens the way to *personhood* in the fullest sense and witnesses to that state.

We can serve the universal, mandatory values of truth, beauty, and goodness like any "objective" cause, and still forget what we are in our innermost *true nature*. Many of those who serve the world selflessly unwittingly sacrifice not simply human nature and the ego's urges and desires, but also true nature and the individual claims and rights that are rooted in it. In other words, it is all too easy to make our essential, subjective being a part of the deal when we set out to do our objective duty.

We may triumph over ourselves, but the freedom we gain by serving "objective" values unconditionally is still a long way from the deepest type of freedom we are meant to have. That freedom comes of a maturity that allows us to yield to the third impulse from the Absolute, the impulse from the all-embracing, all-transcending *unity of Being*. Being free here means that absolute unity enters our own inner being and resolves the fatal antitheses that rule us in the world of the ego. It is only overcoming the antitheses of life and death, absolute and contingent, spirit and nature, timeless values and temporal destiny, worldly existence and otherworldly Being, and fusing them in a superordinate whole, that makes us free in a *personal* sense. True personhood eludes us until we begin to see how opposites can coincide, outgrow the Being/existence dualism in ourselves, and harmonize world-ego with true nature.

But what way must we follow to attain this ultimate humanity that is also ultimate freedom? The way that leads through *experience of the Absolute in our own true nature*. The gateway to personal freedom, to human maturity, is the *experience of Being*, the "Great Experience" of Zen.*

Our "true nature" is the mode in which divine Being is present and striving to manifest itself in every one of us.

---

* Cf. p. 82 below.

We attain *personhood* to the extent that we integrate with that true nature, and so become capable of witnessing freely and consciously to the Absolute in this life. We can experience Being in ourselves only by experiencing our own true nature, and we can find our true nature only in the experience of Being, which shakes and dissolves our ego-centered, worldly existence. And so what really counts is to open ourselves to the inner experiences that put us in touch with a reality totally unlike the reality we construct when we define and understand objectively—the familiar reality that allows us to master "the world." When people ask anxiously whether these are not "mystical" experiences, requiring special talents and essentially "subjective," they are falling prey to objective consciousness, which rules the scene today and finds expression in scientific thought and technical mastery. Absolute experience transcends objective thought, and the sciences have no hold on it—any more than the humanities, with their conceptual and objective bias. This is why the human being as person is accessible neither to science nor the arts, but only to a third branch of knowledge, which we still do not have, but are starting to develop.

The fact that the absolute reality encountered in the experience of Being cannot be defined, explained, or conceptualized does not mean that we cannot speak of it. Indeed we can speak of it and know what we mean, even if we have never experienced it ourselves. Deep in our true nature, we intuit this experience and long for it, and this is enough.

In fact, we all have experiences of Being at certain turning points in our lives, but are usually unprepared for them, and so miss their significance and waste them. We have them when we are filled with joy, but oftener still when we are plunged into sorrow. We have them when we reach the limits of our strength and wisdom, when we fail completely—but are somehow able to accept that failure. And as the old ego and its world let go and fade away, we sense the emergence of another reality within us.

Many of us have experienced the nearness of death—in air raids, illness, or at other times of mortal danger—and have found that if, at the very moment when *terror* engulfs us and our inner resistance collapses, we can somehow submit and accept (doing something that the self-shielding ego cannot begin to understand), we are suddenly calm, our fears are instantly forgotten, and we have the certainty that there is something in us that death and destruction cannot touch. And for a moment we know: "If I get through, I'll know once and for all what I live from, and what I should be living for." We are suddenly, inexplicably conscious of a new and invincible strength. We do not know its source or its purpose—we only know that *we are standing in it*, that it encloses us utterly. This is the sign that Being has touched us, and been able to penetrate our innermost being, because the shell we had fashioned for ourselves—and that cut us off from it—has been atomized.

Anything that pulverizes our imagined independence can bring us the experience of Being (if we only accept it), and so (if we accept it) can the kind of *absurdity* that threatens our sanity—injustice, for example, which brings us close to madness. If we can only give way and accept the unacceptable, we often find, at the very moment of doing so, that Being suddenly gives us a sense of deeper meaning, makes us feel part of an incomprehensible order. A great clarity illuminates us. Once again we cannot say what it is showing us, or what purpose it serves. It is totally inexplicable, and we are simply *in* it, just as we were previously *in* strength.

These experiences of Being can come to us in a third way, when we suddenly find ourselves utterly *alone*—perhaps when we lose our nearest life companion—and facing a *sadness* that we cannot bear. If we then receive the grace to do the impossible, to submit and again accept the unacceptable, we may suddenly feel ourselves caught, surrounded, and shielded by love, even though we cannot say where it comes from, or where the answering love that we feel in ourselves is directed. Like strength and clarity before, it is a state in which we find ourselves—and also, like the others, a state in which we witness vitally to Being, which transcends the whole basis of our previous existence.

People are having these experiences more often than we suppose. But they do not know what is happening, are unprepared for the gift, cannot square it with their old beliefs—and so pass it by, trivialize it, and fail to profit from it. Later they may say that it was just a passing mood, a natural release from unbearable tension. Now, however, they have come back to normal and can see things clearly. The truth is exactly the reverse; it is before the experience and after it that their vision is blurred by rational ways of seeing that hide the truth from them, and prevent them from accepting and recognizing Being in the numinous qualities they have just tasted. This, at long last, is what we must learn to do: recognize these turning-point experiences as windows to the Absolute, and find the courage to accept and serve the reality they show us. Only by doing this can we develop unshakable belief—unshakable because it is not belief "in" an "unknown," but the expression and sign of an *experience* of otherworldly Being that nothing and no one can take from us.

Are extremes of anguish the only path to the experience of Being? Certainly not. These crisis situations are simply those in which Being can unexpectedly touch and seize us most powerfully. Joy also has its turning points, the only problem being that intense worldly happiness is itself easily mistaken for the Absolute. But the spirit bloweth where it listeth, and so, more often than we think, people are suddenly lifted— momentarily or even for hours or days at a time—into a state where the absolute light shines through them. But the realm of objective spirit, in which we see freedom simply as victory over nature, destiny, and dogmatic belief, lacks the richness of inner experience, in which Being's presence alone is enough to make us fully, personally free.

We must learn to make the distinctions that show us that human life is fulfilled in the tension between a worldly reality centered in the determining ego, and an otherworldly reality centered in our true nature and in the true nature of everything else. But we must also see that we cannot resolve this tension by choosing one reality and rejecting the other, but only by integrating the two. The answer is not an "either/or" choice, but wholeness on a higher level. This wholeness is embodied in the *person*—manifesting Being in existence, true nature in the ego-sphere, and the otherworldly in the world, and proving his or her maturity by doing so.

Every step on the path to inner consciousness of Life brings us new riches and new power. But it also brings new dangers and new obligations. The same is true of the transition from objective to supra-objective, from worldly to otherworldly consciousness.

The ego's vision suppresses the absolute center and conceals it from us, and the anguish of being pushed toward the "periphery" intensifies our longing for liberating contact with that center. But our reactions and instincts are still basically worldly, and there is always a danger of wasting the experience of contact by letting the ego take over. When the Absolute first touches us, the great temptations are: *to stop there and to cultivate the experience for its own sake, to relapse into lethargy, or to give way to selfish pride and misuse the forces of the Absolute for worldly ends.*

There are countless people today who have tasted the Absolute, and surprisingly many have been left with the longing (which we all basically have) to deepen the contact and preserve it. This explains the countless small groups and circles in which, with the help of more or less competent leaders, people perform exercises that are supposed to release them from normal consciousness. All kinds of practices are current under such respectable names as yoga, meditation, reflection, relaxation, and so on. But there is a very real danger of maturing and approaching the threshold of change—only to find the door suddenly barred again.

The first danger is that of stepping beyond normal consciousness, dissolving the ego's ties, preparing to make the transition into personhood—and then stopping short and yielding to the pleasures of mere free-floating experience. We should remember the warning words of Meister Eckhart, the medieval mystic: "If, when meditating, you ever enter a state so blissful that you would choose to remain in it forever, tear yourself free as quickly as you can, and seize on the task next to hand; for these are melting sensations, and nothing else!" These "melting sensations" are the very sensations that are leading so many people today to sink themselves in a rapture that dissolves the barriers (e.g., LSD), but provides no impetus toward further change. When this blissful letting go takes over, the way to a form that expresses the Absolute is barred.

There are also many people today who use relaxation exercises, rather than drugs, to find temporary release from the petrified ego, but who then remain in a state that is vague and unfocused, and basically does nothing for them. I know men and women who have exercised for years, who practice daily "meditation"—and yet are further from inner change than many others who do none of these things. When asked why they exercise and what it does for them, they talk about moments of release, suspension, weightlessness—"good feelings," which last for an hour or two at best. But this kind of short-lived *experience* has nothing to do with *change*. And change actually recedes if we forget that this is our real target, and focus instead on simply feeling good. It is vital that the newly opened spiritual energies should also be "cored" in our personal center, since this is what determines commitment to the inner way and the birth of a new conscience. We must also purify ourselves deep down—work properly on our unconscious—for failure to do so endangers all our "successes" on the Way, and makes genuine fusion with our true nature problematical. What I am saying here is that nothing threatens the Way more than the cult of mere experience, in which we slide away from our real task—admittedly a hard one—and surrender to "higher sensations." Of course, every contact with Being has a rapturous quality, and we must not reject that aspect. What we must reject is any tendency to stop at that point and give ourselves over to a languorous, subtle enjoyment.

A second danger is a false, lazy, *unprofitable tranquillity*. Paul Brunton once told me of his impression that many of the yogis he had seen in India were leading people astray by giving them something they were genuinely seeking, but seeking from their egos—lazy peace of mind, the thick-skinned calm that nothing can disturb. Induced inertia of this kind has nothing to do with true spiritual serenity, the vital stillness that provides a perceptible, invigorating, and fruitful link with the divine. It may well make a pleasant change from turmoil and angst, but it seals us off from the creative depths. It is a dead stillness, in which nothing moves. Vital stillness, on the contrary, is a stillness in which nothing is left to impede Life's movement of everlasting change.

Our first contacts with Being should release us from the ego's power, and the third danger is that of reversing their meaning and allowing the ego to feed on them. Charged with transcendent energy, neophytes easily forget that this new inner power is a gift and obligation; they take all the credit themselves, and something that should make them humble inflates their pride instead. In such cases, the gift is not merely wasted, but becomes the source of a perilous megalomania. Its effects are fatal, both on others and on the person who diabolically misuses something given to help him or her serve the Absolute in the service of the ego.

Christian spiritual leaders rightly cite these three dangers—the *sybaritic cult of experience, slothful repose,* and *inflation of the ego*—when they question, or even deny the value of experiencing Being, and of the exercises that bring such experiences closer. In the deep-down element that dissolves the ego and its world, we always run the risk of losing ourselves in an ocean of impersonal release, or triumphantly using its energy to revive the hybrid ego. The danger is certainly a real one, but to conclude from this that the experiences themselves are harmful is to make the mistake of people who reject their old beliefs because so many "representatives" distort them. Reacting like this is a sign that we have never experienced Being truly and fully for ourselves; for every real contact with it in true nature brings not only rapturous release from the dominant ego and its petrified concepts, images, and attitudes, but also, as all of this "dies," the "birth" of a new subjective core and of sterner obligations. Something very special happens when we really make contact with Being, and its meaning is not "experience," but *transformation.*

Our biggest mistake, once contact has been made and the process of change has *begun,* is to assume that we are home and dry. Even the deepest experience of Being still leaves us human, and so partly determined by the ego, which focuses on survival and accepts only the objectively tangible as real. We also retain the personality that would gladly continue to serve and enjoy objective values, and flees the obligation of full personhood because it cannot reconcile transcendent true nature with the here-and-now ego. We can never attain once-and-for-all maturity, any more than we can attain once-and-for-all, God-given peace of the kind we taste in the experience of Being. In every change, an unchanged residue is left to threaten the progress we have made. This is why everything depends on constantly renewing our *commitment* to Being, as we have experienced it—and never standing still is the key to that renewal. Maturing is a matter of setting out firmly on the Way, of committing ourselves afresh from moment to moment, and of allowing ego and Being to merge again and again. Repeatedly overcoming the ego's fear of pain and rejecting its "impersonal" ethic, we must also be prepared to *demonstrate* our loyalty to Being over and over again *from* the uniqueness of what we are personally, *in* the uniqueness of what we are externally.

Maturing means accepting the yoke of a freedom in which we stop willing arbitrarily, and start willing something that incomparably deep experience has revealed to us as our own true nature's ultimate vision and desire. In other words, we are mature when we can be trusted to use our personal freedom correctly.

We are mature when our beliefs are rooted in experience of the Absolute and are constantly reaffirmed in fresh commitment. This is the only maturity that allows us to determine what we are and what we do in a manner that accords with our appointed task: to witness to otherworldly Being in the world.

We are mature to the extent that we attain personhood, accept our experience of the Absolute as real, commit ourselves to it and, on the strength of that commitment, are able and willing to obey the summons and manifest transcendent Being, as we are and perceive it in our true nature, in here-and-now existence. Indeed, Being can be witnessed to only in here-and-now existence. Otherworldly Life appears *in* the world's law of "dying and becoming."

The freedom that maturity brings us is something more than the spiritual freedom that lifts us above the world's limitations. Indeed, being personally free is not a matter of transcending our here-and-now destiny, however painful, but of facing up to and enduring it.

Maturity shows when imminent annihilation and the world's absurdity push us beyond our natural limits and we still stand firm and refuse to betray our true nature. Typically, we betray true nature when we sacrifice everything to safety, prefer a quiet life to necessary conflict, make compliance with codes that are existentially false a pretext for being untrue to ourselves, accept other people only when they side with us and give us an easy time, misuse religion to assume a false humility and shirk the real challenge—in short, whenever we prefer the calm of the surface to the turmoil of the depths, the safe "horizontal" plane to the perilous "vertical" dimension.

Being mature is a matter of repeatedly finding the courage to face up to life's obscurities, to recognize and attend to the commanding stillness in which the other dimension addresses us and, in so doing, see and accept the world as it is. Commitment to the Absolute gives us a new openness to the world, allowing us to take things as they come, see the familiar with new eyes, distrust the whole notion of arriving, and avoid fixed conceptions of the world, other people, and God. Whenever we have to take a definite stand, this commitment allows us to keep the freedom we need to relinquish it again for true nature's sake, turn our back on certainties, and start over.

In all of life's vicissitudes, people who are genuinely mature demonstrate loyalty to Being by focusing on the one, unchanging task that it sets them: witnessing to the timeless in the temporal, the Absolute in the contingent, the otherworldly in the world. Ultimately, they are not concerned with mastering the here-and-now world, or rising above its limitations in an otherworldly spirit, but with making both it and their own here-and-now selves *transparent, in* all their limitations and imperfections, so that the Absolute can shine through them. Repeatedly starting over is the only way of doing this, however, for Being is obscured by fixities and objective concepts, and flowers only in a creatively redeeming process of renewal. In other words, maturity belongs to people in whom the wheel of change turns without ceasing and in whom Meister Eckhart's mighty dictum "God's being is our becoming" fulfills itself in obedience to the everlasting law of dying and becoming.

People who are truly mature are rooted in Being in a way that is not just a matter of belief, but of personal experience, and this shows in their ability to endure things the natural ego cannot endure, accept things it cannot accept. It also shows, however, in an ability to burn the old self repeatedly away in a stage-by-stage process of change. It is this connection with the Absolute that repeatedly allows them to overcome the ego's fear of pain, to avoid taking an easy passage as a sign that all is well, and to endure the world's disharmony without bitterness—suffering from it, but suffering *fruitfully*.

It is not those who fancy that fear, sadness, and despair can be overcome once and for all who are mature, but those who repeatedly find cause, in their anguish at life's abiding insecurity and imperfection, to stop identifying with the timorous, afflicted, and despairing ego, and to melt that ego down in contact with the all-resolving ground of Being. As they do this, a deep, redeeming strength repeatedly fills and renews them, while they themselves increasingly bear the imprint of true nature, are increasingly imbued with a commanding love and—transformed *in* their weakness—are given the strength to endure this life, and grow ever more transparent to a greater Life beyond it.

TRANSPARENCY

When it matures in the right way, human life becomes transparent—transparency being the quality that allows otherworldly Life, present in the individual and in the world, to be seen and sensed through both.

A thing is "transparent" when something else can be seen through it. We might also say that a thing is transparent when it is permeable for something else—when that second thing can act effectively through it. When we say that a person is transparent or permeable in this sense, we are not using those terms as we use them of a window, through which a landscape is seen, or a pipe, through which water flows. In those cases, we are talking of objects that are distinct from, but transparent or permeable to, other objects, which are themselves distinct and permeable.

A transparent human being is not a "what" letting another "what" through, but a "who"—a person who is transparent or permeable to his or her real self. Basically, indeed, the "who" we are is entirely determined by the "who" we can let through, since the one thing that makes us the person we are, overtly or covertly, is the person we are deep down, in our true nature.

To understand transparency in relation to things—a windowpane, a lampshade, a veil, a text, an honest or dishonest face—all we need is eyes and adult common sense. Being mature or immature has nothing to do with it. But to understand what transparency means in human terms—as a personal state of mind, being, and consciousness—we need something more. We need to have reached a certain stage in our human development.* That stage may be innate or achieved. If the latter, transparency marks the culminating point in a development process, and allows true nature's deeper dimension to shine effectively through the superficialities of ego-world consciousness. This kind of transparency also gives us a feeling for something that transcends both the ego and its consciousness—but contributes, deep down, to fulfillment of the ego's real purpose.

Transparency is a state in which otherworldly Life manifests itself in the world, Being speaks in the language of existence, true nature appears in the self, Life's infinite breadth, depth, and height are revealed in finite forms, and things start to glow from within. Once we ourselves are fully transparent, everything we meet becomes transparent too, and other people's true nature is revealed (although this transparency also shows where and how far it is obstructed).

Becoming transparent and allowing our true nature to manifest itself effectively is the meaning, purpose, and result of the self-realization process that we are meant to complete. Transparency is maturity's meaning, and this shows that revelation of something is life's intended purpose. When we are transparent, we are in contact with the world in a way that

---

* Cf. Dürckheim, "Mächtigkeit, Rang und Stufe des Menschen," in *Durchbruch zum Wesen* (Stuttgart-Berne, Huber, 4th edition, 1967).

reveals the unity of Being. There is something in this contact that unconsciously speaks to the true nature of other men and women, bringing it out and making it palpable to them. They feel mysteriously touched, stirred, and summoned in their own wholeness and depth, and also encouraged to show themselves bravely as the person their true nature makes them.

In others, transparency melts everything that obstructs contact with true nature, and so releases a creative, saving energy. It brings blocks to consciousness, and blocked values to light. The persona falls away, and the person emerges. To be transparent is to be permeable to what one really is, and from it. Transparency reveals true nature. It is a transforming force, liberating and life-giving in action and inaction alike. Transparency generates transparency.

The only way of seeing others transparently is to reject objective, analytic consciousness, for which human beings are all distinct and separate. In their true nature, all human beings are connected to the wholeness of Life. Indeed, every human being is this wholeness himself or herself—though only as *one* of the modes in which it can reveal itself humanly.

Taking this further, every human being is one of the modes in which otherworldly Life is attempting to come progressively to consciousness of itself in a specific form. Whenever it does this in us, it gradually releases us from the clutches of ego-consciousness. It is prevented from doing so as long as we identify with the world-ego, rely willfully on ourselves, cut ourselves off from Being, and focus one-sidedly on the here and now. In this state, we are prisoners of the world and, as Martin Luther put it, "servants to all things." We have no one but ourselves to turn to, and this leaves us utterly impoverished. Reliant on our own possessions, knowledge, and abilities, we are cut off from what we really are—and Being's undivided fullness collapses into mere multiplicity.

The creative powers of the deep thin down to a sleight of hand, which we use to conceal our own emptiness in a series of superficial forms. Formal order fades to a network of "relationships," and true nature's absolute unity is reduced to a complex of social contacts.

Severance from Being is our innate, inevitable destiny, and it generates the typically human suffering that prepares us for the coming to consciousness of the Absolute that we have betrayed. We can become transparent only by completing the predestined process in which, impelled by the anguish of estrangement, we gradually open ourselves once again to the Absolute in our true nature.

The transparent self, or goal of our maturing, is that integration of world-ego and true nature in which other-worldly Life is also present in everything the world-focused ego experiences, does, and leaves undone.

Promising, commanding, and coercive, otherworldly Life is constantly at work within us in the language of our own true nature. It is precisely this that shows that inner "true nature" is not a figment of the imagination, but can be experienced as the mode in which a superhuman force speaks and operates within us. The farther world-ego parts us from true nature, the more we can expect to sense it one day in the suffering caused us by the world. When that happens, it may come home to us as absolute conscience and commanding summons to conversion, and also as a power that promises salvation. At this vital turning point we may even be given the grace to experience true nature in ourselves—witnessing to the Absolute in its transcendent fullness, order, and unity.

Being transparent means being able to *perceive* true nature in ourselves, and also being able to *let it in* as a world-transforming power. True nature's promise must be heard, but so must its summons to change. For this, we need a special kind of sensitivity—the extrasensory kind that allows us to sense the otherworldly in certain *qualities* of experience. Developing this sensitivity is one of the central elements in all initiatory practice.* It marks the beginning of the conversion process that affects us in a total sense, turning us from a personality focused on the world into a person open to the Absolute.

Because we ourselves "are" the otherworldly in our own true nature, our consciousness is also equipped to perceive it. But our "reason" is off-key, and must be "retuned" so that the Absolute can ring out clearly. This retuning process is initiated by the pain of a state in which our "metaphysical pores" are blocked. To clear them, we must leap to a new kind of consciousness, in which we experience reality in a new way, while a wholly new dimension opens before us, with its own significance, order, and logic. This leap is what experience of the Absolute is about, and contacts with the other dimension can pave the way for it.

Transparency is not simply a state in which we perceive Life, having once been cut off from it, but also a state in which Life perceives itself in us. It is the Whole's revelation of itself to itself in human consciousness, and in the polarity of ego and true nature. To the extent that we can sense and admit absolute wholeness in this way, we experience ourselves as microcosm, and take the first step toward becoming a universal man or woman, in whom otherworldly Life expresses itself with ever-growing purity. At this point, we ourselves *are* that Life—and, thrusting repeatedly forward, it now bursts from the ego/true nature antithesis as a new, deep dimension of consciousness, leaving objectivity and polarity totally behind.

Growing transparency marks progress on the path of self-realization. To realize ourselves in this sense is to connect

* Cf. p. 109 ff. below.

with our true nature, and to become conscious of the Absolute in it as something beyond the world and at the same time in the world. In this process, we become ourselves—not simply as the expression of true nature, but as the integration of true nature and world-ego. Personal transparency depends on this total, integrated state, in which we are transparent in the world-ego to true nature, and capable of witnessing to it in the world. The mysterious, unifying force of the unfolding self is focused on this overall state as active potential. To be transparent is to have the blissful—and commanding—ability to realize that potential.

We cannot understand what transparency is until we have experienced it, however briefly, as a state, or at least have enough of it in ourselves to sense that achieving it is our real purpose in life.

We experience transparency as joyful or commanding contact with true nature, and as promising intimation of a new relationship with the world—a relationship totally infused with the Absolute's intensifying presence. The otherworldly irradiates the world, dispelling its objective limitations and allowing it to open up, release its creative potential, and touch us on the deepest level, where we are linked to it.

When we make the move from the world-ego stage to the truly personal stage of consciousness, we find that the world-ego/true nature antithesis can be fruitfully *resolved* in transparency—but must not be dissolved by facile selection of one side or the other.

As long as we remain focused on a world that can be perceived and organized objectively, we can be sure that our true nature will eventually reach a dead end and start choking for air; for it belongs to the otherworldly sphere, and cannot fulfill itself in this one. And yet it is precisely the pain induced by this one-sided vision that eventually wakes us to our true nature. We are first aware of it in an inexplicable inner turning away from the world, but register it properly only in the mysterious fullness and power we experience when our normal strength and wisdom actually collapse in some shattering crisis. Sometimes, too, it comes out of nowhere, for no special reason—simply because "the time is right." When we wake in this way, we are aware for the first time of being fully transparent to something beyond our normal, worldly experience—something that we call otherworldly or transcendent. But this *instant* of joyous *awakening* must be followed by the *change* to a state of mind and being in which transparency becomes a permanent condition. We are always inclined to make the mistake of believing that our first contact with Being—in itself an overwhelming experience—actually transforms us as well.* In reality, it simply marks the first step on the great and agonizing Way that, repeatedly plunging us into darkness and remaking our whole personality, slowly leads us closer to our goal.

Our "true nature" cannot be explained in terms of other things, traced to worldly factors, or classified and understood "psychologically." On the contrary, it is itself the supreme classifying principle, and holds the hidden key to the whole meaning of human life.

The world always wants us to be sensible and efficient, and it also expects us to play a reliable, productive role in serving the community and upholding certain durable values. True nature, on the other hand, tells us to evade the world's clutches, to open ourselves to it only, and to live for it alone. If we followed its urgings to the letter, we would ultimately escape the world completely, and cease entirely to belong to it. But human beings who reject the world and fuse with the Absolute in this final sense are no longer human. The longing to do this is an "Eastern" one, and there is something of it

* Cf. Dürckheim, *Erlebnis und Wandlung* (Stuttgart-Berne, Huber, 1956).

in all of us. But realizing ourselves in a specific worldly form is our task as Westerners and, while this remains our goal, experiencing union with the Absolute is not incompatible with "being-in-the-world," but is actually the essential precondition of being-in-the-world *in the right way*. This experience itself is only the first stage of integration with the Absolute, i.e., the process of change that makes us transparent.

As long as we see Being and true nature simply as the world-ego's opposites, we remain the prisoners of objective consciousness. Leaving that antithesis behind is the fruit of the process of becoming that turns us into a person, in whom world and true nature are so closely integrated that the world-ego becomes increasingly transparent to true nature, which becomes increasingly apparent through it. In this parallel development, the mediating element and the thing it mediates come steadily closer to coinciding in the person, who transcends the poles. People who reach this stage can truly say: "The eye that sees me, and the eye with which I see, are one and the same eye."

The ego clings to fixities, prevents otherworldly Life from coming to consciousness, and stands in the way of transparency, but all of this ultimately demonstrates Life's *cunning* (as Hegel put it, "The spirit's way is never straight"). Life is trying to achieve awareness of itself in human beings, but can manifest itself only in and through a *counterform*, which lends it relief. Light, after all, needs a reflective medium to be seen. This is why every step toward hardening of the ego, which is turned to the world and away from the Absolute, threatens final severance from Being—but also increases the chances that the anguish caused us by widening of the gap will make us open ourselves to the Absolute consciously. Of course, this possibility depends on our resisting the temptation to try to approach the Absolute dawning within us by the very means that separate us from it. For us in the twentieth century, this means that rational consciousness will not help. Neither will even the most determined heightening and refining of the ego's potential and actual ability to conceptualize life and master it technically. We can approach the new horizon only by taking the leap into a new way of experiencing ourselves as subject and the world as reality. Push it and refine it as we may, objective thinking can never gain a hold on something that cannot be objectively apprehended; something that lies beyond normal consciousness cannot be grasped by means natural to that consciousness. No microscope, however powerful, can *show* us the echoes of the Absolute—we must *hear* them. At some point in our lives, what we need is a radical transition into a new way of being human, a genuine transformation on the path of maturity. The change that this brings is even more dramatic than the change that occurs at puberty—but there is, in some sense, a link between them.

At puberty, we discover our own sexuality, discover ourselves as men and women. The unquestioning wholeness of childhood collapses in the painful experience of fragmentation, of sexual division. But against this background there awakes a new longing for wholeness, and also a sense that loving union of the sexes is the only way of becoming whole again, and at the same time fully ourselves. It is at the very point where the I/you tension first brings us a sense of the whole that transcends them both that true nature opens within us.* Here, as in the tension between the personal forces of deep-down true nature and the objective counterforces of the world, we sense it as the underlying meaning, potential, and task of existence. In our own self's language and voice, we feel "the whole" as promise and premonition of a possible fusion of world and true nature. Who can forget the first

* Cf. Dürckheim: "Der Aufgang des Wesens in der Zeit der ersten Reife," in *Durchbruch zum Wesen*, op. cit.

glimmering sense of one's own dawning individuality that makes puberty a time of near-despair, and yet gives it a lonely and joyful radiance! And that surging of the heart that tells us of a better world, in which the cold systems shaped by adults, which have nothing to do with what we really are, give way to a new pattern, forged by the transforming fire of the Life we feel deep within us.

In puberty, we become aware not only of sexual dualism, but also of the contradiction between a world that insists on objective achievement, and an inner principle that summons us to subjective perception. The reason for today's rebellion of the young is the old one: The fixed systems and supposed realism of their elders are forcing them to deny the reality of something that is emerging within them—something totally their own, inexpressibly deep, and indeed of ultimate importance. But just as adolescents first recognize the world's harsh, self-generating systems by contrasting them with their emergent true nature, and first see that true nature plainly by contrasting it with the world that denies it, so adults today (if they have reached the requisite stage) are rediscovering absolute true nature through the suffering caused them by the very world that threatens their humanity. Conversely—since we would otherwise end by romanticizing the Absolute or pursuing an Oriental cult of redemption—the genuinely mature are also rediscovering the world; for the world itself is becoming transparent and allowing true nature to show through. Similarly, experiencing true nature fully makes people transparent to the world in a new way, and open to its real meaning, as something that obliges them to manifest the Absolute, and at the same time offers them the opportunity of doing so. The potential transparency of the here and now is revealed to them, and they realize that they themselves have power to manifest and shield the Absolute in the contingent. When we talk of manifesting Being "in the world," we do not simply mean in the special situations created by special experience, but also, as absolute conscience develops, in everyday life. The only way of doing this, however, is to escape from the ties of a world that reduces us to objects into the *personal* freedom we attain when true nature becomes a permanent, indwelling presence.

But if everything we are, think, and do in everyday life is to be transparent, then we must become increasingly transparent to ourselves. It is at this point that the circle, which opened and started to bring Life to consciousness in puberty, closes. If true nature opens within us, and we feel that we are identical with it, we can also feel that we are witnessing to Being—even (and especially) in the ego-role we play in ordinary life. In this way, we can remain true to Life's primal unity amid all the divisions of existence. Indeed, our coming to awareness of this unity and witnessing to it in the world may eventually help us to see that all the divisions and tensions are actually intended to focus us on unity. This realization may then bring us the awareness of wholeness in which we finally outgrow the anguish caused us by sexual dualism. Once we have attained maturity and experienced supra-antithetical Being completely, we may reach that state of primal unity in which, while continuing to behave, think, and speak as men or women, we leave dualism behind, experience the human condition in its suprasexual (androgynous) primality, and sense that we may ultimately be able to express that quality and give it form.

The human state of transparency is one in which the person—and specifically the person in relation to the contingent world-ego—allows absolute true nature to show through. One could also say that the person who, as world-ego, is only part of the whole, becomes a window for the whole behind it.

In "what-consciousness" (objective), we perceive the

contingent and the Absolute as separate and opposite realities. When we become aware of ourselves and of the world in "who-consciousness" (subjective), we can still speak of the contingent and the Absolute—but we now mean something different. At this stage, they are experienced as two modes of the self, and the tension between them is the mode in which we experience ourselves and, through ourselves, Life. The contingent is thus present in our experience of the Absolute, just as the Absolute is also present in our experience of what we call the contingent.

When we speak of transparency in "who-consciousness," we mean the person as clear medium for true nature. The more transparent we become in this sense, the more true nature expands within us, while the world-ego progressively surrenders its autonomy until it becomes a pliant medium. Increasingly, it feels itself imbued with a deep-down something that explodes its limitations and compels it to obey. In this way, it progressively becomes an extension of true nature, while the world-ego/true nature antithesis shifts into a polar relationship. In the same way, the antithesis of "who" and "what" consciousness develops a productive tension and becomes consciousness of Life in the person, who senses in the tension the wholeness in which he or she lives.

The quality, depth, and duration of transparency are variable. The consciousness that stands between us and the truth may be either strong or weak, and may become permeable for shorter or longer periods. The triggering force may be outside events or inner changes that penetrate the ego's tidy system. A minor breakthrough, a fright, an instant's happiness, a sudden upswing—any of these can briefly bring transparency. Events may take a turn that surprises us, momentarily upsetting the whole pattern of our lives and confronting us with a new reality. For an instant, we sense that a new dimension is opening before us. We do not know what it offers, or what it wants of us—and we are frightened. Our automatic defenses come into play, and the wave of Life, having lifted us for an instant, dies out on the sands of the old, familiar system. It is our ability to cope with the totally new that sooner or later determines whether the Absolute can reveal itself to us and transform us progressively. We all have a certain freedom to heed the summons of the deep within us, or allow our natural defenses to take over; to follow the call, or resist it. We are all afraid of the depths of the unconscious, and of the shadow—not our own shadow, but the shadow of excluded Being.* What we fear in this shadow is the sudden eruption of Life unlived and suppressed, Life turned malevolent and threatening. And yet true nature cannot genuinely open until we encounter the shadow, just as the shadow does not really appear until we have genuinely experienced true nature. The aggression packed within the shadow is actually less of a threat to our whole accustomed existence than the Life that stays blocked until we leave that aggression behind. This is why we are deeply reluctant to let in that Life—which is only waiting for a chance to reveal itself—and fear of it makes us cling to the shadow that conceals it.

The kind of transparency we have is determined by the stage we have reached in our development.

There is primal, prepersonal transparency, in which Life still shines out unchecked. This is the child's transparency, and something of it survives through all later stages of consciousness. It is expressed in a "yes" to life that underlies and unconsciously accompanies all our experiences. Otherworldly Life is also present in this "yes" as sustaining power and promise, as the basic tone of the overall harmony, at the heart of every state and stage of consciousness. But when our au-

* Cf. p. 114 ff. below.

tonomy hardens to a point where this basic tone falls silent, the Absolute's deep-down, "animating" force disengages. In effect, we lose our souls. When "yes" becomes "no" without our being aware of it, the ground starts to crumble beneath our feet, and we find ourselves fighting for air. Angst takes over—choking sensations and vertigo, as if we were falling headlong in a vacuum. Alternatively, without any obvious reason, exhaustion, melancholy, or nervous confusion may set in. But it is precisely moments like these that may suddenly show us the underlying quality of our own experience, and make us sense its total negativity. Indeed, with the right kind of sensitivity, we can even experience the agonizing presence of otherworldly Life in its very absence—in the unmistakable, deep-seated pain that we feel at severance from it. A numinous quality clings even to negation, and it is this that seizes many people on the deepest level, allowing them to find their way back from "no" to "yes."

Absence of the basic, affirmative quality that typifies normal feeling for life is a part of all depression. Its victims appear to have lost their drive, while their inner light seems extinguished, and the thread cut that normally connects them with the Absolute. Conversely, real transparency invariably points to the presence of that inner affirmation that, as vitalizing breath and impetus of life, is a basic part of every fulfilled life-consciousness.

The degree of our maturity determines whether the fullness, inner form, and unity of Being, which transparency reveals, merely color our experience without our realizing it, or are registered, brought to consciousness, and recognized —just as guiding people to maturity involves teaching them to sense the three aspects of Being in the world around them.* When we "recognize" Being, we are not, of course, defining

* Cf. p. 110 ff. below.

it objectively in the world-ego's sense—but are subjectively recognizing, accepting and, as it were, joyfully assenting to a wholly new experience. Though wholly new, it is also strangely familiar—so that we suddenly feel completely at home and at ease in it. This means that, meeting the world in the right way, we become transparent to ourselves, and respond to Being's touch by answering simply from deep within ourselves: "Yes—you are it. Yes—that is what you are. Yes—*that* is what *I* am."

Otherworldly Life is present at every stage of worldly life, and expresses itself in the language of that stage. As we develop, our perceptions of the Absolute are changing all the time. The differences are determined both by our innate stage and by the stage to which we have matured. Every level of consciousness has its own prismatic range and shows us Being's light in its own colors. At every stage, however, we live "deep down" from the innermost heart of our true nature, from Being. Of course, consciousness means that we, unlike flowers and animals, cannot do this directly, and are always more or less resistant, but it also offers us the chance of working through this resistance and someday experiencing the Absolute consciously. This is also the meaning of the tension between joy and sorrow, fulfillment and yearning, compulsion and duty, constraint and liberty, which distinguishes us from other creatures.

For us, here-and-now life is never simply life, but experienced, remembered, and anticipated Life, and the otherworldly is inherent in the "feel" of all worldly experience. Counterpointing ordinary consciousness, it speaks to us as basic harmony, premonition, longing, promise, enigma, fear, hope—and often, too, as "imminent joy." It summons us at those overwhelming turning points, when all the barriers collapse. And it also calls us unexpectedly, for no apparent reason—gentle as breath or vivid as lightning—in the midst of everyday life. But it undoubtedly calls loudest when something tears us from our normal context, when panic seizes us, when extremes of joy or sorrow carry us beyond ourselves, or when we risk everything in combat, love, or celebration. The more our ordinary consciousness develops, the more we entrench ourselves behind forms and systems that seal us off from Being. But the more our maturity increases, the more we concentrate on reaching a state of mind and being in which the Absolute does not merely speak to us briefly, but in which we become transparent and sustain unceasing inner dialogue with it.

"Transparency," says Jean Gebser, "is the form in which the spiritual manifests itself."*

There are people who are highly intelligent, but who are not spiritual. What do they lack? Transparency. Even sophisticated intelligence is still no guarantee of spirituality. It is strange how any attempt to discuss the "Way" with people who are intellectually brilliant, who may even have had philosophical training, but are not transparent, inevitably fails. They simply do not know what is being talked about. Once they start to suspect, they turn cynical or angry; for opening themselves to the Way and accepting the ultimate reality it shows them would put an end to their complacency, which is solidly based, but totally worldly.

What is the difference between art and kitsch? Kitsch lacks transparency, and remains cloggingly on the surface. Art, on the other hand, always embodies the tension between the contingent medium and the Absolute it mediates, and allows something totally beyond form and nonform to resonate as counterform in a formed artifact. This is why unspiritual people, however cultivated and intelligent, are often

* Cf. Jean Gebser: *The Ever-Present Origin* (Athens: Ohio University Press, 1985).

boring. The merely intelligent find the spiritual dimension disturbing—after all, it casts doubt on everything they stand for. This is also why ordinary citizens, enclosed in their suburban comforts, are often made uneasy by artists—and why there is nonetheless something about artists that attracts and fascinates them. Mysteriously alluring and yet faintly threatening, real Life, which they have repressed, speaks to them in it.

Therapy that is merely concerned with easing pain or restoring worldly function can never make us transparent. Once we start seeking, we can attain transparency consciously only on the way of initiation, the way on which the soul penetrates the mystery and on which Being, illumination to Being, and transformation from it are the only things that count. To find ourselves, however, we must first be converted, and this means passing through the darkness—our own darkness, in which Life rejected, squandered, or lived against its own law has taken refuge. What is needed here is total change.

There are people who already know about transparency, who not only intuit and yearn for it, but who seem to be very close to it—and still cannot reach it, for they are not prepared to enter the darkness that goes before experience of the Great Light, beyond light and darkness. There can be no "resurrection" without "death and damnation" first.

For the light to dawn, the element that screens it must first disappear. However, this concealing element is not simply a wrong "way of thinking," not simply a complex of mistaken images and ideas. It is, rather, everything we are, everything that ingrained notions and attitudes make us, everything we become by identifying with *one* "way of being in the world," in which we are so firmly and comfortably embedded that we confuse it with our "self-being."

On the way to our fixed worldly form, we invariably silence things that want to speak, restrain things that want to be free, and repress things that want to live. Until all of this surfaces plainly—even if that means sacrificing our accustomed system, and regardless of the cost—we cannot make the decisive leap. As soon as we start to sense transparency as our real target, we must die to ourselves as the fixed, obstructing element. Spiritual acrobatics are no use to us here—no merely imaginary leap can take us to the goal. The ego must "die" so that true nature can be "born," and we ourselves become transparent. This is true of any contact with Being that is more than momentary. It is also true of our first experience of the Great Light. To start with, however, this experience is no more than a promise. Fulfillment of that promise depends on utter change, the kind of change that shows in permanent transparency. We can attain it only by plunging into the shadow-world and losing ourselves in its somber depths, *having first* seen the light. It is precisely at this point, when the flower of Life seems within our grasp, when its colors dazzle us, its scent makes our head reel, and we feel that we have only to reach out and pluck it, that we must turn away and stop trying to seize it directly. Again and again, we must confront our shadow, for we can earn the right to change decisively only by facing up to the forces of the deep, being seized by them, and thus seeing them for what they are, and making them a part of ourselves.

Real transparency, in which Being bursts out once and for all as the light that dissolves all the darkness/light antitheses, depends on a death died in absolute darkness. This death is preceded, however, by that initial encounter with the light, in which we first experience liberation from the world-ego and the torment it inflicts on us. This experience transports us out of ourselves and into the otherworldly, and we may be tempted to try to hang onto it, but it then brings us the experience of a "darkness" that can no more be "psychologically" explained than the light that freed us to start with. It is not until we have encountered both light *and* its opposite that we can see the ultimate light that waits for us, beyond all antitheses, in the innermost heart of our true nature.

In our first encounter with Being, we dissolve in the radiance of deep-down redemption and, perhaps without knowing what is happening, experience the joy of being transparent for the first time. We feel liberated from the threefold anguish of constantly having to do battle with the dangers, absurdity, and cruelty of the threatening world around us. We may also feel that an immense light is illuminating us and sweeping us into the warm, pellucid, and invigorating flood of a mighty, redeeming Life. Anyone who meets us in this state is instantly aware that we have changed. And yet this state is still not the "great transparency." That comes only when, having woken to the Absolute, we experience it in its dark, as well as its bright, aspects, and again experience the despair of separation from it—perhaps, indeed, *really* experience that despair for the first time. It is only in this dark night of the soul that the Absolute really comes home to us, makes us over and allows us to realize our humanity in the world, instead of sublimating it in ultimate, otherworldly transparency.

It is only at this point that our existence takes on a form in which the Absolute does not merely touch us and depart, but stays with us as a permanent, harmonious, effective inner presence, waking the absolute potential in everything around us.

The transparency that concerns us here is transparency to the Absolute—in human terms, transparency from the Absolute and for it in a consciousness grown permeable. The Absolute always manifests itself to human beings in its three essential qualities—fullness, form (order and regularity), and unity. As the emphases shift, it may therefore speak to us as gladdening, invigorating, elemental contact with the forces of the cosmos; in the creative energy of comprehensive, in-dwelling images and laws that direct us on the deepest level; or in the language of the soul, which allows love to enter and in which the union of heaven and earth, ego and world, and ego and true nature manifests itself creatively and redeemingly in a human heart. This heart is not, of course, the "normal" heart, which is focused and dependent on the world alone. That heart must pass out of being, sink into the purifying depths, re-emerge, and open itself to the powers of the divine before it can conceive and bring forth the true human being, in whom the Absolute becomes an inner presence and can manifest itself in the world.

Being is overpowering strength, shaping energy, and light, and it reveals itself in transparency, sometimes in one of its three aspects—fullness, order, and unity—and some-times in another.

In each of those aspects, the way in which it touches us is conditioned by our own maturity. But its presence is really, mysteriously felt and apprehended only in the alter-nation of the three modes in which it speaks to our human senses. Indeed those senses are themselves one of its modes. And so its becoming an inner presence in its three modes is not simply a matter of its being perceived by us, but to some extent a matter of its encountering itself in our consciousness. In this self-encounter, it manifests itself humanly—and so acquires redemptive and creative force for those of us who have become ensnared or lost in the self-assertive windings of objective consciousness.

When Being comes to inner consciousness as plenitude, transparency brings a sense of its endlessly overflowing pres-ence. People who have this transparency seem to feel the divine impetus, the redeeming, creative, sheltering, and re-newing powers of the deep within them. They experience all of this as boundless potential, forcing its way into them and exploding their existing form. And when their experience of Being is a true one, it bears no relation whatsoever to their situation in everyday life. Indeed, this is the hallmark of total transparency—the experience of Being that it mediates has no contingent correlatives. It is precisely when we are poor, helpless, and weak that we experience the fullness of Being as power, wealth, and energy. In the same way, Being often reveals itself to us as order and meaning at the very moment when the world's senselessness is edging us close to despair, or comes to us as all-embracing, all-protecting unity when we are utterly abandoned and alone. To be truly transparent is thus to overcome the world's dangers, absurdities, and cruelties, and to overcome the fear, despair, and sorrow they inspire in us. One might even say that transparency to otherworldly Life is born of the death of worldly life—and of worldly life's medium, the ego. This is true as long as we live—and totally so when we die, and Life's glories open to receive us.

In transparency, regardless of anything that happens or is done, we experience the coming of otherworldly Life to effective worldly form as a special *radiance*, in which it reveals itself—and always in a specific true nature's language.

The heartwarming radiance of the young provides one example. The radiance of a young girl, for instance, who moves naturally and innocently through a world of which she still knows nothing, and yet is filled with the sense of a Life that is still no more than a promise. This radiance shows most powerfully when defining consciousness is just starting to draw its veil of ignorance across the watching soul, and Being develops a special brilliance as the shadows encroach. Once worldly knowledge takes hold and experience hardens to a fixed, objective system, true nature's light grows pale; for "grasped" existence obscures it, and "growing up" and losing oneself to an objective world also means growing away from the light. The starlight of true nature fades in the daylight glare of worldly consciousness.

All objects and living creatures—plants, flowers, trees, stones, and also human beings—have a certain radiant quality, something that seems the emanation of a fine-spun material reality. Its nature is determined by the object, creature, or place in which it inheres, and so is the feeling that that object, creature, or place conveys. It varies from the living to the dead, from the old to the new, from the sick to the healthy. Every color, too, has its own particular radiance, and this helps to determine atmosphere—the welcoming feel of a living room, for instance, as compared to the clinical feel of a laboratory. Sensitivity to all these types of radiance also varies from person to person.

Transparency's radiance is something else again. In it, Life itself touches us—always in a different language, but always in the same tone. Always, too, it has a special purity, freshness, and depth. It is as if Life's eternal youthfulness, which transparency allows us to perceive, were showing itself to us. The most moving example of this is undoubtedly the radiance seen on the face of someone who has just died—an otherworldly glow that seems to reflect the light of infinity. And then comes the shattering transition to the state of really being dead, of being a corpse. The dead person seems to collapse, grow smaller, sink inward (the corpse is no longer the person). Transparency vanishes, and a lifeless body is left—waxen, stiff, and dreadful, silent within and silent without. And in this collapse, we sense corruption and decay.

Radiance is Being's presence, which total transparency allows us to experience directly. This radiance can never be pinned down to a definite time or place. It lies outside those dimensions, and this is why the consciousness that defines and clings to particulars can never perceive it. Because they do not "see" it, the prisoners of objective consciousness say that a dead person looks "calm" or "peaceful"—and so remain firmly on the finite surface. The majesty of Being, which rules and transcends the here and now, is being realized before them, but their eyes are closed to its sovereignty. Its radiance reveals itself only when true natures meet. And this is why, when contact is made, it touches and speaks to us on the deepest level, and we feel ourselves summoned and present in our innermost true nature.

"Radiance" is one of the modes in which Being shows itself to us, but there is also a false radiance that comes from the ego and usurps true nature's place—a satanic glitter, which blinds without illuminating. It is often very like the true radiance, and yet it is utterly, fundamentally different. To distinguish the true light from the false, we must be in living touch with our true nature. People still in thrall to the world-ego are easily led astray by the false light, which always has an alluring, seductive quality. But it is cold and heartless. It seems to hold a sparkling promise, but the promise is deceptive, lying, shallow and empty.

This deceptive radiance sometimes marks people who were born in a special sense to be bearers of the light, but have themselves usurped the Absolute's place and prevented it from breaking through. The space that divides them from their true nature has never been purified, but is sealed off by the ego. They remain unfulfilled, and their "radiant" look is penetrating and at the same time voracious. Behind apparent fullness, we sense poverty and emptiness; behind seeming conviviality and warmth, we feel something cold, uncommitted, and remote, and the chill of an unrelieved solitude. And yet people like this—with their bright eyes, flashing teeth, winning ways, and lying smiles—are often irresistible to others.

When we are finally, utterly transparent, we are totally free—in the way that true nature makes us free. Nothing divides us from ourselves or others. When we have this absolute freedom—when we stand, even for an instant, in the freedom of true nature—Being illuminates the whole world, and illuminates us with it.

Experiencing transparency as manifestation of the Absolute does not depend simply on the Absolute's light, but also on the darkness of obstructing human consciousness. It is only because we ourselves *are* the light in our true nature, and at the same time are *separated* from it by ordinary consciousness, that we can forge a new consciousness against the background of the old one, come to awareness of the Absolute in it and reach, *in* this awareness, a new developmental stage—the stage of being transparent. But none of this is automatic—far from it.

On the way to personhood, our transparency does not increase unless we work hard on ourselves all the time. Insofar as transparency means manifestation of the Absolute, this work is initiatory* in character, since its concern is with contacting, experiencing, and witnessing to the Absolute.

Growing transparency depends on progressing (or "leaping") from the analytical to the holistic, from the static to the dynamic, from the objective to the subjective, and from the personal and worldly to the suprapersonal and otherworldly mode of conscious experience and conduct.

Permanent transparency demands total *change*. This change may be sudden, or may start as a gradual process, finally coming to a head in an instant. Always, however, it means a more or less painful letting-go of habitual ways of being and forms of consciousness, and transition through a mighty darkness. Repeatedly, the old must die an agonizing death before the new can be born.

Although it is generally true that humanity today (and

---

* Cf. p. 74 ff. below.

particularly Western humanity, which faces paralysis from its own fixed systems) is evolving toward a new stage of consciousness, this is far from being a process that the rising generation can expect to complete without effort. The young are spared neither the anguish of reaching the barrier and trying to break through it, nor the transitional shock in which the old self dies. There is no shortcut through the dark no man's land that lies between world-ego and true nature, and there is no way, once true nature emerges, of avoiding the transforming conflict with the world, which reveals its full powers at this point. Those young people who embody the future today—and not all young people do that—have a racking inner sense of a necessary transition to a new stage of consciousness, a transition that is forcing itself painfully on them and insisting on being *experienced* in the full, subjective sense, *gone through* regardless of all obstacles, and *completed* in an agonizing process of genuine change. This change, however, is not just an inner process, but takes in the body as well.

Once we have genuinely tasted true nature and know both what transparency can do for us and what it demands of us, we are eventually bound to discover the body's significance as mirror of knowledge and means to personal transparency.

In fact, the way in which we normally regard the body today is one of the results of one-sided, objective, world-focused consciousness. Objectively, we see it as a more or less independent entity, and contrast it with the soul and intellect. Subjectively, we are usually aware of it only when it hurts or refuses to perform. Basically, our only concern is to keep it pain-free, vital, and productive. As long as it *functions* and obeys, as long as we are "healthy" (productive and well-adjusted), the body does not really "exist" for us consciously. It interests us only as an instrument of safe, smooth, and relaxation, a simple letting go that prevents any form from emerging.

Without permeable form, or formed permeability, in the body, transparency remains mere wishful thinking. A typically modern example of what we have in mind here is physical tension, the kind of painful *tension we often feel between the shoulders*. Reading that last sentence, many modern "intellectuals" will probably have an uncomfortable sense of being dragged down from the speculative heights to the lower concerns of the body. All of this, they assume, is a matter for doctors, teachers of gymnastics, and masseurs, but not for spiritual teachers, who travel or point to the inner Way. This reaction is typical of those who confuse the body we are with the body we have, and the mind with some disembodied spirit, and treat the development of consciousness as a purely inner process. Of course, perceiving tension across the shoulders only in "what-consciousness" turns it into a merely physical symptom, something that hurts and reduces our efficiency. This "physical" problem then demands a "technical" remedy, and indeed an injection or massage can remove it, at least temporarily. This tension means something utterly different, however, when looked at in "who-consciousness." It then means that the sufferer is personally there in a manner that unequivocally contradicts the Way and blocks transparency, that his or her attitude is one of avoidance, self-protection, defense, caution, and mistrust. This "hunched-up" posture points to domination by a world-focused ego, which feels threatened by the world or unable to meet its demands. Being ruled by that ego is the central obstacle on the way to transparency, and an equally potent obstacle is the overall state that embodies that condition. This insight offers us a possibility, still largely unknown in the West, of working through the "body" toward personal transparency.* But before we can do this, we must develop the sensitivity we need to perceive the body from within as the mirror and medium of the person progressing toward transparency. Coming back to our example, we must learn to see that "stiff shoulder" from within as expressing an attitude that blocks the way to transparency. Eliminating this and other wrong attitudes is always a matter of becoming "properly centered,"** and we also need to do this to develop the "right" state of mind and being, which breaks the self-protecting ego's spell and allows us to become transparent to the true nature that is struggling to reveal itself in us. This makes us permeable to the movement in which the wheel of change rotates unceasingly, and also ready to let Being, which is present in our own true nature, enter the world as experience, radiance, and effective force. It is only when this movement becomes permanent that the worldly form that matches absolute form is realized in it.

* Cf. R. Peltzer: "Die Arbeit an der Transparenz über den Leib," in M. Hippius (ed.) *Transzendenz als Erfahrung* (Weilheim/Obb.: O. W. Barth, 1967).
** Cf. Dürckheim: *Hara, the Vital Centre of Man,* translated by Sylvia-Monica von Kospoth and Estelle Healey (London: Unwin Paperbacks, 1977); "Wann ist der Mensch in seiner Mitte?" in Tenzler, *Die Wirklichkeit der Mitte, Festschrift für A. Vetter* (Munich: 1963).

FORM

Knowing the world conceptually and mastering it technically, living without pain, and realizing the ideal in the real—all of these are eternal human aspirations. Our perceptions of human beings themselves are conditioned by whether we see them as objects of knowledge, as suffering creatures who deserve our compassion and assistance, or in terms of their longing for self-realization and harmony. The perspective in each case is different, and so are the things it shows us. Each of the three emphases has its own vision and approach.

The first is essentially concerned with knowing objectively, with noting facts, tracing them to causes, or relating them meaningfully. This is the scientific approach.

The second is concerned with relieving suffering. This is the sphere in which doctors, therapists, and pastors operate. Achieving their goals depends, both in theory and in practice, on a compassionate, understanding approach to others in their worldly bodies.

The third is concerned, however, with people who are evolving toward an outer form that matches their true nature, with people who need guidance and companionship on the way to maturity—that is, transparency.

Broadly speaking, these three emphases reflect the divisions and disagreements that exist between the various groups who are working on human beings today. The situation is one in which different ways of seeing, which actually belong together or complement one another in terms of the whole, are divided or mutually hostile. Often—as if we had three competing souls—all these ways of seeing are present within us at the same time, as sources of mutual tension and disruption. Often, too, people with particular axes to grind use one to disparage the others.

Particularly when it is purely theoretical, the "psychology of consciousness" taught at our colleges in the wake of a great tradition is highly, and regrettably, reluctant to accept the findings of practical psychology—for example, the insights of depth-psychology (psychology of the unconscious) derived from therapeutic practice—or accepts them only when they can be squared with recognized problems and existing conceptual systems. We need only think here of the disdain with which C. G. Jung was treated in his lifetime by the "official" schools of psychology. Conversely, practicing doctors and therapists often complain that "college" psychology is useless when it comes to helping and healing. There is also a third faction that claims that neither consciousness theory nor depth-psychology, solely geared to relieving the anguish of worldly malfunction, is relevant to becoming oneself from one's true nature. This third group is itself attacked by others, for whom maturing in accordance with true nature's law is a secondary concern, and certainly not part of everything we are and do. People like this are particularly suspicious of the further claim that genuine maturing is rooted in the Absolute, and that we must recognize the connection and make it a conscious part of the process before we can become fully, personally mature—for traditional science has no hold on any of this. Indeed, transcendent experience and insight are always uncomfortable, both in what they are and in what they imply, for the proponents of theories and practices that center on surface "phenomena," or minor therapies that seek to restore worldly function or simply ease pain. Ultimately, however, any way of working on people that restricts itself to definable, conceptualized, surface phenomena, and lacks the courage to push its "empirical" approach down to experiences that transcend both the "psychic" and the "physical" is bound to prove sterile.

Any effort at knowing, healing, or leading that really concerns the whole person must start with those experiences that affect human beings on the deepest level and allow the otherworldly to ring out in them. This is the only angle from which a person's outer form at any given moment can be properly seen and judged, as a mode in which otherworldly Life, present in his or her true nature, is able—or unable—to manifest itself in the world. It is also the only basis on which people can be genuinely helped and guided toward realization of an outer form that accords with true nature and their own inner form.

Every living creature embodies the Absolute within it in its own way, and realizes it more or less completely, depending on the conditions in which it has become what it is.

The outer form that the Absolute achieves in human beings is a special one, and is conditioned by the fact that every human is a conscious being, and is meant to become a self-conscious, world-conscious "subject" or, more accurately, "person." The vital nerve in this subject is the tension between absolute Being, forcing its way toward manifestation of itself in true nature, and a particular here-and-now form. The relationship is expressed in a painful tug of war between contingent, worldly obligation and absolute, otherworldly duty

—and in the sense of a freedom powered by the Absolute, which can finally outgrow and overcome the contingent. Human beings are special because they are not simply trapped in a network of systematic causes, but are part of the Absolute, and thus destined for this freedom and capable of finding it.

We all exist in a definite, limited, here-and-now world of conditional factors that threaten our outer form's survival and saving links with true nature, make fulfillment of ourselves and our world problematical, and imperil our oneness with ourselves and our surroundings. And so the inner and outer circumstances in which our outer form is realized together maintain a steady tension between that outer form (the body) and the inner form we are meant to manifest totally and purely. Externally, human life is an ongoing struggle between inner form and outer. Internally, this same struggle is the theme of our maturing.

From childhood on, circumstances and other people exert a combined pressure that suppresses, distorts, and obstructs the development process dictated by true nature. This is why our outer form at any given moment is never the direct projection of Being within us, but is also the product of those other shaping factors that prevent us from realizing true nature's inner form directly and completely. And yet we are all permanently driven by an urge toward the Life-form embedded in our inner nature. Merely surviving is not enough—we all want to live ourselves out and fulfill ourselves as a definite someone. And basically, whether we know it or not, we always want to develop in a way that allows us to witness totally to otherworldly Being in worldly existence.

When we talk about true nature, we mean the way in which every human being individually shares in otherworldly Being, and otherworldly Being strives to manifest itself in him or her—or better, "as him or her"—in the world. From this innate true nature, people feel an unremitting urge, a vital sense of moral obligation, and a permanent longing to realize themselves in a specific form, in which (their) Being can reveal itself clearly in existence. The prerequisite here is, however, total harmony between what they "are" and aspire to be primally (that is, from their true nature), and what the here-and-now world allows them to become. In the midst of change and development, in tension, duty, and the longing for definite form, there is always something that remains one, unique and real. We call it *inner form*—meaning true nature as the innate law of becoming that orders us on, shapes our basic aspiration, and unwaveringly drives us toward achievement of a specific outer form. It exists in every one of us, and demonstrates its reality in its uncompromising insistence on being realized and witnessed to in a specific outer form under *all* circumstances—whether it speaks as life-instinct, inflexible conscience, or ever-present longing.

There are outer factors that prevent all living creatures from witnessing directly to inner form, but human beings are hindered by inner factors too. There is nothing in plants or animals to prevent inner form from assuming outer form in a manner that accords with Life's law and with their own true nature. As they grow, ripen, and bear fruit, they simply allow their inner shaping principle to take on outer form—the form in which they visibly, physically exist. Every human, however, also seeks and possesses, achieves or misses outer form as a conscious being, as a particular person who, wittingly or unwittingly, assists or inhibits that process.

For us, self-realization is not automatic, but an active, cooperative response to the summons "I have called thee by thy name; thou art mine."* That name—the name that belongs to us alone, and in which we hear the personal call—imposes certain obligations on us. It is only by accepting those obli-

* Isaiah 43:1

gations and answering true nature's call that we become a person through whom Being—shaping and binding, redeeming and creating—can ring out. Outer form is not something we are given, but something we are *given to realize*. It is only by cooperating consciously in the process that we can realize it, and achieve transparency.

What do we really mean when we speak of a human being's outer form?

We mean his or her inner form's way of "being there" in the world. This involves both the inner and outer man or woman—not just the visible, physical body, but the whole person as the living total of the gestures in which he or she experiences, lives out, and "embodies" himself or herself.

In the world, our outer form can only approximate to our inner one. It would, of course, be ideal if outer form allowed us to display inner form purely, manifest it humanly—that is, consciously, freely, and in pure gesture*— and sustain it. Gesture is pure when it witnesses purely to true nature. Attaining this purity (total transparency) is the purpose of all exercise, and particularly exercise that involves the body.

The concept of "outer form" is slightly misleading when transferred from objects to humans, since it conjures up the notion of separable bodily form, which can never give an accurate picture of the form in which humans realize themselves bodily. Objective consciousness stresses the visible and tangible, and so naturally limits our conception of human form to "surface appearance," which seems to stay the same from one moment to the next and so lures us into a static way of seeing. Geometrical notions of "perfection" or "completion" (e.g., the perfect circle) also naturally color our ideas on the

---

* Cf. Dürckheim: "The Healing Power of Pure Gesture" in *The Way of Transformation: Daily Life as a Spiritual Exercise*, translated by Ruth Lewinnek and P. L. Travers (London: Unwin Paperbacks, 1980).

form that we ourselves are expected to realize. Thinking about human form in these terms betrays the influence both of objective consciousness, which is obsessed with fixities, and of the unique emphasis that Westerners place on "bodily perfection" (we need only think here of the masterpieces of European classical art, whereas the East has hardly ever portrayed the body for its beauty's sake alone). The biggest mistake we can make in trying to think correctly about human form and perfection is, in fact, to borrow our concepts from objects and art and apply them to living human persons.

Whenever we think of human beings as "things" with static qualities, or visualize them in those terms, we miss their essence—as we do when we confuse "Life-form" with the ordinary body. The "Life-body" also contains the whole of a person's "inner form," the form of his or her inwardness—in short, the *whole* of his or her personhood, insofar as it takes on form.

The static way of seeing human beings usually extends beyond the way they look, and includes their *true nature*, which is also thought of as a kind of fixed form, with a kind of size and shape. This is where countless misleading, wrongheaded ideas have their source.

A person's true nature and "inner form" are a part of the absolute reality. The normal mind has a natural tendency to contrast the Absolute with the here and now—which it totally transcends—and to see it as something eternal, fixed, and immovable. But this conversion of limitless, transcendent Being into something that "lasts forever" and "stays the same" in a temporal sense (contrasting it with here-and-now transience) is just another typical expression of the stage of consciousness at which the defining ego's dualistic vision predominates. Also, the Absolute never takes on worldly form in any final sense, but assumes form only to shed it again in a never-ending process. This is why we must never think of inner form as something fixed, but as the "formula" that governs true nature's efforts to manifest itself in a worldly process of becoming.

The Absolute appears in here-and-now entities as the inner law behind the process of change that constitutes their real character. This is why living creatures can never express Being truly in a complete and static outer form, but only in a total state in which true nature's law of becoming is securely anchored. Eckhart probably put this best in his masterly phrase: "God's being is our becoming"—meaning that our true nature can manifest the divine only in movement and fluidity. This would make the ideal outer form one that matured and altered without ceasing, thus allowing Being to manifest itself ever more clearly and purely in our individuality, and leaving nothing to obstruct the *process* of change, which is its only way of doing so. It is precisely here that taking on form causes problems for us, since the "fixities" that block any process of becoming are decisively part of our makeup. Our real business in life is to change without ceasing and, changing, to witness reliably to Being—but the nature of our consciousness permits that only to a limited degree.

For us, "being there" in the right way means being there in the right way as a human being, that is, as the vehicle of a human consciousness. It is precisely as conscious beings that we must not be closed to Being, but in tune with it. The only route to this goal, however, is the indirect one that leads through development of a consciousness in which we circle fixed points and ourselves harden into stasis. It is almost a part of our human nature—and this separates us from the animals—that we start by trapping, enclosing, and pinning ourselves down in fixed structures. And it is only emergence of the ego at the center of these structures that makes us truly human. But this hardened world-ego is at odds with the otherworldly Life within us, and we do not attain outer form that matches the inner one until our "ego-form" allows our true nature's aspiration toward becoming to show through. This process is a long one, and is filled with renunciation and sacrifice—for things that have come into being must be surrendered repeatedly. It is governed by a law of becoming—and so the "right" outer form is in fact a preordained series of necessary stages. Ultimately, the right outer form is a *way*—a way that we travel in harmony with our true nature.

And so, when we say that a person's outer form is transparent, we do not mean that an image shows through it, but that it reveals the "way" written into his or her true nature as a necessary sequence of developmental stages. Fundamentally, inner form is the way written into our true nature, the way we must follow to fulfill ourselves.

Circumstances and self-assertive instincts can make us "conform"—take on forms that are not really ours and contradict true nature's law. Whenever these forms become ingrained, they provoke both mental and physical disorders, for they have somewhere brought the "wheel of change"* to a halt and prevented us from maturing in accordance with our true nature. Whenever they take a firm and final hold, these "substitute solutions" and artificial forms lead to those permanent disorders that we call *neuroses*. To the extent that neurosis results from clinging to existential forms, we are all neurotic. Our actually becoming ill depends on how far true nature's shaping energy is blocked. This is where the difference between slight and severe neurosis lies.

The things that come to light when deep-seated neurosis is healed (and often make neurosis the first step in the great process of changing and maturing) can tell us a lot about human beings and the Life-form intended for them. In fact,

* Cf. Dürckheim: *The Way of Transformation: Daily Life as a Spiritual Exercise*, loc. cit.

the barrier that impedes and finally distorts Life in the neurotic is merely a dangerously heightened version of the normal consciousness that is centered in the defining, "fact"-obsessed, self-shielding ego.

Like everything that expresses what we are, these "attitudes" are also present or absent in our bodies. As we mature on the path of self-realization, we develop a fine inner feeling for the extent to which our bodily existence is meeting the demands of inner form or falling short of them. Our gestures, body-tone, breathing, and overall posture all faithfully show where we stand in relation to heaven, earth, the world, and ourselves. Typically, people are bodily "right" when they can engage the world without "tensing," and can also accept it and let it impinge on them, just as it is. Why? Because they are transparent to their own true nature—in other words, open to perceive it and capable of witnessing to it calmly, cheerfully, and kindly in the world, regardless of circumstance.

The process of change that accords with true nature affects the body too. The voice becomes more resonant, the complexion slightly darker, the expression of the eyes both fuller and deeper, the movements rounder, their whole rhythm more relaxed and also crisper; the body's overall tone becomes more balanced, the breathing changes, and the whole posture becomes more permeable and acquires a new center of gravity, in which the whole person (and not just the body) is correctly centered. But this new or heightened sense of the "rightness" of our outer form also allows us to sense, with increasing acuity, the extent to which we are substantially, and not merely physically, in tune with true nature—for the "substance" of physical form also changes when this is the case.

The human condition also has an inner form, but this is not the same as the inner form that seeks to realize itself in the "right" outer form in individuals. It aspires, too, to a definite Life-form—but we see it only when we accept that inner form can never be totally realized, indeed that being human means that perfect form can never exist in any final sense. There are three reasons for this: (1) the process of maturing and bearing fruit is a never-ending one; (2) ego-world consciousness, which aims at permanence, is seeking all the time to subvert the ever-changing form demanded by true nature; and (3) the human body grows and sustains a thousand injuries in the here and now, and so can never "match" the Absolute completely. These are inescapable facts, and we are mistakenly idealizing and distorting "right form" if we let our notions of "formal perfection" blind us to them. We must assert our here-and-now reality, accept ourselves in it, face up to the burden of contingency and all the errors that go with it—and still pursue perfection tirelessly. In other words, we are not truly on the way to "right form" until we both try to follow true nature's law of changing and becoming *and* have the humility to accept ourselves in the form that life brings out of us at any given moment.

The *individual*'s inner form is realized in the here-and-now body to the extent that it overcomes that body and transforms it. The *human condition*'s inner form is realized when, without faltering in our pursuit of perfection, we accept our here-and-now body, just as it is, and allow it to become transparent to Being *in* its here-and-now contingency.

We said at the beginning that there are three urges that focus our attention on other people: the urge to know, the urge to help, and the urge to perfect (expressing itself in guidance on the Way). When we find the form that really matches our own inner way, all three acquire a deeper significance, for they all become channels for otherworldly Life's revelation of itself in our here-and-now lives.

Consciousness anchored in the otherworldly brings a

higher kind of knowing, in which our awareness of ourselves and of the world extends to Being, and allows it to become fruitfully operative as "higher insight." Similarly, compassion learns to distinguish between the anguish caused the ego by the world and the anguish caused true nature by the world-afflicted ego. Finally, guidance leads us toward fulfillment of our true vocation, which no longer appears as a matter of realizing a supposedly independent ego, of liberating and redeeming the individual—but of liberating the Absolute in the individual. Transforming our basic energies like this and making them serve Life is the meaning and purpose of the *Way* —the Way that we call the "Way of initiation."

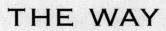

THE WAY

OVER THE THRESHOLD

THE EXPERIENCE OF BEING AND BELIEF

Today we are witnessing an event of universal significance in the history of human development, an event the consequences of which we cannot yet foresee: For the first time, the West is starting to open itself to initiatory experience all along the line.

What does this actually mean?

Religious *belief* in a transcendent divinity is today being joined by a religious sense of the inner Way—the Way that derives from *experience* of otherworldly Being, sets out to transform the individual through *practice*, and culminates in a liberating *awakening* to the Absolute. Belief in an infinitely remote God, and in a redeemer who closes the gap, is being joined by the knowledge that we can wake to an otherworldly Life within us, a Life that we ourselves are on the deepest level and in which we have never been unredeemed. We can—and this is what the West is now starting to realize— follow a law written into our own evolving nature and gradually fulfill the conditions that make this waking possible. This new religious instinct is nothing more or less than following of the Way, innate in our true nature, to full personal maturity. It starts with the experience of our true nature and leads through recognition of the conditions on which that experience depends, to awakening in the light of a higher consciousness—all of it through a disciplined process of exercise that brings us step by step out of the night of natural consciousness.

"Initiation" refers to a human dimension that differs both from ordinary "religion" and from any kind of "therapy."

This dimension belongs to a definite *stage* in human development, the stage at which we first see that our own and the world's real nature is not the nature that natural consciousness takes to be real. For the natural ego, things are real when they present themselves to it in a physical, here-and-now sense, can be known and mastered to a greater or lesser extent by rational consciousness, and contrast "objectively" with "subjective" inner states, which are ruled by urges and feelings. When we reach the stage where the Way of initiation opens before us, we see that this vision shows us only one aspect—the ego-world aspect—of another, true, otherworldly reality.

The natural vision, which makes people identify with the world-ego, also makes them see themselves subjectively as distinct and separate from the world around them—and from anything beyond it. At the same time, they have a natural sense of being dependent on the world and on otherworldly forces that transcend their normal understanding (and are therefore termed "transcendent")—and determined by them. They need these otherworldly forces to endure the pain of living in the world, and believe in them in the forms and images that embody what mighty prophets of the Absolute have said in their particular spiritual tradition. Religion at this stage develops as belief, and forms a kind of counterpole to natural consciousness; for transcendent reality is transported into an external, superhuman dimension, where it becomes an object of faith. This faith is not based on personal experience, but on the words of intermediaries, to whom certain things have been revealed—or on special inspiration or metaphysical speculation. The divine and the human realities are separate—as they are, for example, in the Jewish, Christian, and Islamic religions.

Once everything that transcends natural consciousness is projected into an outside dimension, people are left the prisoners of their natural human condition. It is as if anything else were not their business—except in special states and in the case of "mystics," who go beyond the limits of the properly human. At best, these special states are relegated to the margins of both ordinary and religious life. The whole picture starts to change, however, once these states are no longer projected outside the human sphere, but seen as experiences that come at a certain stage in human development and provide a higher *knowledge*.

The fact is that we *can* experience a supernatural reality that lies beyond our natural ego and normal understanding, and even seems to contradict them. When we experience it, it stops being merely a matter of belief, and becomes a matter of *knowledge* instead. The experiences themselves are more common than we imagine. When we reach a certain point in our development, they are no longer rare and intermittent, but thoroughly familiar, and give us a sense of commitment to the reality they show us. But how can we be certain that all of this is genuine, and that we are not simply the victims of illusion or wishful thinking? How can we know that these experiences are really experiences of another dimension—genuine experiences of the Absolute?

1. They have a totally distinctive *taste*. *There is a special, numinous quality* that unerringly points to the presence of another reality in human consciousness. There is no way of

describing or classifying this quality—no word, concept, or image can convey it.

2. They have a special *radiance*, which always points to the Absolute's presence in the experience of Being, in the aftereffects of that experience, and even in prolonged contact with Being. It can be perceived both by others—if they have the slightest sensitivity—and by the person concerned.

3. They *transform* us. The extent of the change that occurs, begins, or is caused when we have an experience of Being is the surest sign that the experience is real. Both our *endurance* of the world and our way of *working* in it are affected. In both, the change appears in that lasting transparency that makes others transparent as well.

Even contact with Being (or perception of the "numinous") may well make us ask how we can know that *Being* is involved. One answer to this question runs as follows: whenever we feel physical pain, we automatically assume that something is causing it—even though we know that some pains are imaginary and have no organic causes. In the same way, we automatically assume that all our sense experiences —seeing, hearing, touching, smelling, and tasting—are caused by something, even though we know that hallucinations are possible. Why then, when we have unique experiences, which affect us uniquely, should we not—even allowing for the possibility of error in this area too—assume that "something" is speaking through them or causing them? The inhibitions we feel in the presence of even the deepest experience of Being show how rigid, dismissive, and limited our normal conceptions of reality are—and even more clearly how *frightened* we are of questioning those conceptions, which may well be narrow, but are also well-worn and comforting. The time has come, however, to tear down the barriers that scientists, psychologists, and even theologians still raise whenever experiences of this kind are linked to an otherworldly reality that appears in them.

The validity and implications of any experience of Being can be assessed only by those who have had that experience themselves and felt its effects—but not by those who have never been down that road, or whose loyalty to a fixed system of belief prevents them from taking it. Many Christian believers, for example, have these experiences, feel their redeeming and transforming power—and back off in terror because they cannot square them with their existing beliefs. Blatant materialists can have them too, and reject them for much the same reason. In fact, there is something of the believer and the materialist in all of us—experience of the Absolute always contradicts both some previous belief and our natural understanding.

Genuine experience of the Absolute brings us a knowledge that turns our natural world- and value-system on its head and sets another in its place. All the basic categories of the old system are suddenly wrong. At this point, we enter a state of transparency in which the old, anguished questions—what? where? when? why?—are left behind, for they can tell us nothing about Life. When Being comes home to us, and is neither recontoured and reified, nor amorphously dissolved, in objective consciousness, but remains transparently, wakefully present in subjective consciousness, we attain a new freedom. As a result, the three sources of existential anguish—annihilation, absurdity, and solitude—become doors to higher Life, deeper meaning, and greater security, to a "supernatural" process of development. Something opens up behind all the everyday antitheses, absorbing and resolving them. Life and death, too, are absorbed in a greater Life that bridges the gap and reconciles them. But where is the reality of this greater Life located? Only somewhere out there—outside ourselves?

THE ABSOLUTE WITHIN

The experience of Being holds the key to the Way because it shows us that absolute reality is not something of which we are only marginally, intuitively a part, but something that is present within us, in our true nature—indeed, that we ourselves *are* this reality in our true nature. In short, the experience is decisive because it brings us knowledge of the *Absolute within*.

At a certain stage in our development, we lose our fear of these experiences, stop dismissing them as hysterical, ambiguous, or unhealthy, and cease looking "humbly" for a "cure" that will give us back our peace of mind and return us to our confines—and start accepting them instead. Only when we do this do we enter on the path to full human maturity, acknowledging that the absolute dimension (previously, at most, an object of belief) is part and parcel of our own reality, and that the here-and-now dimension (previously considered the only reality) is merely an aspect of the whole —merely the form assumed by the absolute reality within us when it passes through the ego's unsubtle prism and arranges itself in the ego's category system.

Today we are starting to grasp the thrilling fact that the reality revealed in absolute experience—a reality previously contrasted with the "objective" reality of science and technology, and dismissed as mystical and subjective—is the reality that counts for the human individual as person. Rationally known, "objective" reality, on the other hand, appears as a concealing element, is losing its old dominance, and must be relegated to its proper subordinate position as we move forward on the path to Life.

Of course, the old ego is still there, and still sees the

old reality—although we ourselves now "see through" that reality, and know that the ego conditions and limits it. To the extent that we stay anchored in the ego, we also retain our old habit of projecting the Absolute outside ourselves. But this old way of seeing is no longer fundamentally valid for us as persons. We are "experienced" and we know that the ego necessarily sees transcendent reality as something "outside," although it *is not* outside. Indeed, we know that the inner/outer antithesis is itself conditioned by the ego. Of course, we are constantly relapsing into ordinary consciousness and its way of seeing, which screens reality from us, but we know that we are capable of breaking the ego's bonds—and indeed have a duty to do so. Every step on the path to this freedom can strike off one of the old shackles, but the necessary prelude to each is surrender of what we have and the dying of a new death. Again and again, we must relinquish the subjective self with which we have identified, and all the possessions, defenses, pleasures, and meanings it clung to. Previously, this kind of letting go was entirely bound up with an *ethical* imperative—the need, for example, to sacrifice ourselves or our possessions for an idea, cause, or community, or for "God's" or "Christ's sake." Now, however, the connection is with the Absolute within—the Absolute that gladdens, summons, and commands us in an experience we cannot ignore.

As we advance on the Way of initiation, our lives are progressively filled with this wholly new element, and the more the horizons open up before us, the more we experience the whole thing not simply as *liberation* from the confines of a supposedly natural state, but as a totally new *obligation* to serve an entirely new master. In traditional religion, we served a distant God, but we now experience this service as joyful possibility and absolute duty in ourselves, in a way that turns *obedience to belief* into *obedience to experience*. It is no longer a matter of saving *ourselves* or finding personal salvation, but of making room in the world for the otherworldly Life we have experienced—or manifesting Being in existence.

In terms of ordinary life, all of this is quite extraordinary. Indeed, everything that happens in the experience of Being, as well as all the rigorous stages that lead up to it and all the changes that come after it, center on something that defies normal understanding and is thus *mysterious* to anyone who is unaware that this experience exists or is not yet mature enough to have it. Only those who have been left ready by reaching a certain stage and completing a personal process of maturing—ready for initiation by Life or a master into the meaning, preconditions, and implications of this experience —can penetrate the mystery. The Latin word *initiare* means "to open the way to the mystery."* *Initiation* is the process, and the initiate is someone who not only possesses secret knowledge, but has been transformed by experience, exercise, and trial, and has entered a superhuman dimension of Being. We should use the word *initiation* in this sense very carefully. The event it denotes is so shattering, and so utterly beyond our normal limits, that all its implications are necessarily shrouded in secrecy and hidden from those who have no right to approach it. This respect must be maintained—but the time has now come for human beings to start moving toward this ultimate goal, to follow an "initiatory" path.

Initiation in the full sense is an experience that very few people can have, but many are called to the way that leads to it. And so we use the word "initiatory" to denote things that essentially point to initiation, but are still not identical with the events that occur, the demands that are made, and the mysteries that are revealed on the highest level. To this extent, we can speak of different stages in the process:

* Cf. Julius Evola: "Über das Initiatische," *Antaios*, Vol. V, No. 4.

initiation in the strict sense, which is limited to individuals and closed groups, and is closed to outsiders, and the "initiatory" in the broadest sense, which concerns anyone who matures to a point where Being can be experienced, and that experience made the basis of work on the self and personal change. The term "initiatory" then denotes not just the possibility, but also the obligation, of working to overcome the limitations of natural ego-world consciousness once that stage has been reached. What this involves is making the transition to another dimension of the real, a new form of humanity.

The emergence of the initiatory is one of the great and hopeful portents of change in our time. It is felt whenever poeple are guided by others. If the "guide"—whether teacher, doctor, pastor, therapist, or some other "authority figure"—is an "insider," the guidance that he or she provides will always allow for the possibility of initiation.

If we use the word "religious" to mean anything that connects human beings to an otherworldly reality and brings order, meaning, and hope into their lives from that source, then the initiatory life is a religious life—although the religion in question is not one of belief, but experience. Strange as it may seem, both belief and experience can be—indeed, normally are—present in the same person. Being human, we necessarily tend to identify with the natural ego, and to experience ourselves in a reality in which everything presents itself to us in accordance with that ego's ordering and shaping principles. This is why we also project the divine outside ourselves. Once we reach the stage of being able to experience the otherworldly in our true nature, however, we oscillate between seeing belief in the "Absolute outside" as regression to a lower stage in our development, and knowledge of the "Absolute within" as transgression of our proper limits. This indeed typifies people on the Way: they are already the person they will be, and no longer the person they still are. This is why they can, for example, pray to an infinitely remote God, in comparison with whom they are mere specks of dust, and at the same time sense the divine presence as the otherworldly reality that is part of them in their own true nature. They can believe in Christ the Redeemer, who died for them on the cross and in whom "all things are made," and also experience Christ as their own innermost center.* Not merely enduring these antitheses, but recognizing them as essential aspects of our own true nature and development, is a part of being on the Way—the Way on which the antitheses themselves progressively disappear.

Once we have the maturity needed to enter the Way of initiation, we are summoned to follow it. We have no alternative—it is, in other words, the only way in which *we* can become and remain completely healthy. But the kind of health we are talking about here is not the health that concerns normal therapy.

INITIATORY GUIDANCE AND THERAPY

Recently, a distinction has been made between minor and major therapy, "minor" therapy being the kind that sets out to heal neurosis, to cure mental illness—to restore the patient's ability to get on, get things done, and get along with others in everyday life, eliminating angst, guilt, and loneliness in the process. This whole approach is geared to the needs of

* Cf. Dürckheim: "Wann ist der Mensch in seiner Mitte?" in *Wirklichkeit der Mitte—Festschrift für A. Vetter* (Munich: Alber, 1968).

people who identify naturally with the world-ego, and will always be primarily a matter for doctors. Attention is now focusing, however, on something else as well—something that comes into view when it is realized that the sources of physical or mental suffering can extend beyond psychology's reach and into the heart of metaphysical true nature, into those unconscious depths where the numinous is sensed—always a sign that the Absolute is involved. In such cases, "healing" is possible only if the "sick" person learns to think in terms of that dimension and to see worldly problems as a sign that a self-fulfillment process, in which transcendent true nature can emerge, is being blocked.

Obviously, analysts who lack the necessary maturity themselves are unwilling or unable to acknowledge the reality of a "transcendent center," and dismiss anything that comes from it as the fantasies, illusions, or wishful thinking of an escapist ego. A great deal of harm is done in this way. People who are suffering and who belong at the initiatory stage are seriously damaged if they are misunderstood and even compelled to remain at the natural stage—just as they become sick if, having reached the initiatory stage, they fail to develop in the manner it demands. One could also say that they have taken guilt upon themselves and must pay the price for doing so.

It is important to realize that the change that counts on the Way of initiation does not always begin with clearly defined experiences of Being, with dramatic upheavals in extreme situations. It is sometimes ushered in by more or less fleeting contacts, or even by the breath of the numinous sensed in a dream. Today, however, increasing numbers of people, many of them very young, are starting to notice moments like this and wonder in amazement what they mean. They are lucky indeed if they encounter someone who can confirm their decisive importance, explain what they mean, and reveal the hidden treasures and obligations they contain. All too often, however, these experiences are still belittled and dismissed—in puberty and even childhood, by unsuspecting parents and teachers, who simply smile and shrug them off, and later by therapists, who are inhibited by science, pragmatically oriented, or themselves immature, and so put them down to illusion, exaggeration, sublimation, or wish-fulfillment. In doing this, they are robbing life's decisive moments of their metaphysical value, instead of bringing their significance to consciousness. Noticing these moments and attending to them can be the first step on the way that leads beyond therapy, but this is not necessarily the case. It is true that "major" therapy is not primarily concerned with worldly capability, with helping people to function smoothly and painlessly, even at their true nature's expense—but with self-realization from that true nature. But even major therapy does not necessarily mark the transition to initiation. That comes only when painless compliance with the world's demands and mere *self*-realization from true nature both cease to be the point—and the "real self" is seen as the medium for *Being*'s expression of itself in the here-and-now language of a here-and-now person's individuality. The emphasis here is on Being, rather than the person. Indeed, initiation begins only when the individual stops seeking "his" or "her" self, and is ready to seek maturity solely for the purpose of serving the Absolute. Life does not become "initiatory" until it serves the other dimension unequivocally. As long as contact and fusion with the Absolute are sought for the sake of the self and its welfare, the purpose of the quest is still merely therapeutic. It is only when the process of self-realization is accepted *for Being's sake*, regardless of cost, regardless of pain, and regardless of the loss of worldly capability that acceptance may entail, that the first step is taken on the Way of initiation.

The extent to which depth-psychological insight and

even psychotherapy are needed on the Way is another question. Depth-psychological purification of the unconscious is certainly a necessary part of the process. Without it, we easily fall prey to our constant illusions of being closer to the Absolute and closer to manifesting it than we really are. Like registering the numinous and taking it seriously, recognizing the things that divide us from the absolute reality revealed in the numinous is an important part of the work we must do on the Way of initiation. On the other hand, the right kind of psychotherapy can also—by focusing on the patient's *true nature*—launch a development process that leads to initiation. Religion rooted in belief can do the same, whether the triggering element be belief profoundly experienced, or the anguish caused by loss of faith.

EAST AND WEST

ZEN

The Way of initiation has always been the religious Way of the East. And so, at a time when people in the West are maturing toward that Way, it is hardly surprising that Eastern wisdom and practices should be exerting a special attraction. Today, this is particularly true of *Zen*, the basic teachings and practices of which are by no means relevant only to Easterners, but have the same initiatory significance for Westerners with the right maturity.* Zen embodies wisdom—in other words, its theoretical foundations reflect the experience of mature men and women, who have broken through the world-ego's shell, tasted Being, and witnessed in their own lives to the possibility of its becoming manifest in the world. Through everything Zen is and says, there runs the golden thread of experiences that are not merely Oriental, but of universal human validity—experiences that any human being can have on the way to maturity. Much of this seems Oriental to us only be-

* Cf. Dürckheim: *Zen and Us*, translated by Vincent Nash (New York: E. P. Dutton, 1987) and *The Grace of Zen: Zen Texts for Meditation* (New York: Seabury Press, 1976); H. Enomiya Lassalle, *Zen, der Weg zur Erleuchtung* (Vienna: Herder); Hugo M. Enomiya, *Zen-Buddhismus* (Cologne: J. P. Bachem, 1966).

cause these experiences and their "Way" have never been acknowledged in the Western intellectual tradition. Incomprehensible to rationalists and "suspect" to theologians, they have never been given a chance to prove their value.

Zen writings owe their power to the radiant energy of the experiences that witness to the Absolute, and to the promise inherent in descriptions of them. Abstracted from Eastern tradition and reduced to a few sentences, the general human principles that underlie the teachings and practice of Zen are the following:

1. In their true nature, human beings are one of the modes of divine Being.

2. What they *are* in true nature is concealed from them by what they *have* in consciousness. They are alienated from Being as long as they remain the prisoners of objective, natural, ego-world consciousness, have not been liberated into the subjectivity of Being in consciousness, and have not entered on the path of ongoing change that leads to absolute freedom.

3. All alienation, and thus all typically human anguish, derives from identifying with an ego that pins experience down in fixed images, concepts, and values, and is always intent, in theory and practice, on finding a "secure position."

4. If all suffering is ultimately due to alienation from Being by this ego, then relief ultimately depends on escaping from its power and categories, fusing with the true nature it conceals from us, and thereby attaining a new subjectivity. Being *cured* in this sense means *breaking through* objective consciousness, which is anchored in the defining ego, and *waking* to a new consciousness. This breakthrough*—a process in

* Cf. Dürckheim: *Durchbruch zum Wesen* (Stuttgart-Berne: Huber, 4th edition, 1967); *Im Zeichen der Grossen Erfahrung* (Weilheim/Obb.: O. W. Barth, 2nd edition, 1958).

which the old ego is absorbed into the real self and a new one emerges—is *satori*, the "Great Experience" of Zen. It gives human life a wholly new direction, and is the focal point of all Zen's spiritual guidance.

5. Genuine satori means two things: a shattering, gladdening, liberating *experience*, and the birth of a new *conscience*, that is, a sense that we are in duty bound to effect a change that is the meaning of that experience. The experience itself is that of waking to our *true nature*, and it illuminates us in a way that both frees us and imposes obligations on us. True nature is nothing more or less than the inner *Way* to a state of personhood in which we are transformed and become transparent to the Absolute. Satori thus releases us from the old system, remakes our consciousness, gives us new insight, generates a new subjectivity, and points us toward total change. When real, it is no mere emotional experience, but the starting point on a Way we must travel responsibly toward realization of the subjective state in which our ego is remade and we demonstrate union with our true nature by serving Being in the world. To do this, we must develop a new consciousness, and must change *in the body* as well. Our new bodily state is one in which we are not simply on a new inner course, but have become physically transparent to the Absolute and capable of sensing and witnessing to it in the here and now. This is why Zen also has a natural concern with transformation of the body. In all of this, however, it is not specifically Oriental, but expresses a universal human possibility and duty, and provides a perfect example of initiatory practice.

Eastern wisdom and practices, and particularly Zen Buddhism, are overcoming all obstacles and gaining ground in the West, and this brings us repeatedly back to the relationship between Eastern wisdom and Western intellect. The central issue here is the relationship between the belief-based religion of the West and the "initiatory" religious feeling of the East.

Where do the Eastern and Western spirits meet? They meet in the realms of political debate, world economic development, ethnology, and, above all, comparative religion. Indeed, the encounter of East and West is becoming an increasingly important feature of any attempt to attain a satisfactory world order today. The encounter with the spirit of the East is also becoming steadily more prominent in the searchings of the many Westerners who have lost their old beliefs and are struggling to find a new direction. Whenever the Eastern and the Western spirit are discussed in all of this, "East" and "West" are immediately given geographical references, the East usually being identified with India and Asia, the West with Europe and the United States. The time has now come, however, to look for East and West in a wholly new quarter—*in ourselves*. We should stop seeing the tension between what we call the spirits of East and West merely as a political, economic, or ethnological problem, and start seeing it chiefly as a polar tension in ourselves—where it becomes an inner problem for all of us to solve. We can form a better idea of what this means by reminding ourselves of what we all know today about the relationship between "female" and "male":

There are men and there are women. But there is also a female element (principle) in men, and a male element (principle) in women. We now know that a man becomes fully a man, and a woman fully a woman, only when each becomes *whole*—when the man recognizes, admits, and integrates the female element in himself, and the woman similarly recognizes, admits, and integrates the male element in herself. In the same way, Westerners and Easterners will not become whole human beings, or develop fully as whole Westerners and Easterners, until each side learns to recognize, admit, and integrate the other in itself. Wholeness, whatever form it takes, is the only basis for ongoing, creative human development.

THE UNIVERSAL MAN AND WOMAN

"Human wholeness"—we can intuit what this concept means by thinking of "humanity as a whole," but can ultimately understand it only by looking into ourselves. All the peoples of the earth have their own ways of feeling, thinking, and behaving, but there is nothing in any of them—however remote and exotic—that we cannot find in ourselves, and that does not have its place and value in our own makeup. When we take "primitive" and "civilized" races and peoples, and compare them, we are actually looking at different *stages* in human development. We carry all these stages in ourselves,* and the *"alien"* is also potentially a part of us. And so the things we register as totally alien ("Oriental") in the East are also potentially in ourselves. It is only bringing this potential to consciousness that makes us realize that human *wholeness* is trying to manifest itself in and through us in a very special way—and that we can and must make this possible.

This idea—that of the "whole human being," who manifests the "fullness of Being" in a lengthy development process, under constantly changing circumstances and in infinitely varied ways (but always in humanity's language)— has all the creative force of a primal archetype, and makes us

* Cf. J. Gebser: *The Ever-Present Origin,* op. cit.

aware of the *universal* man or woman innate within ourselves as something real. As humanity's starting point and destination, it shimmers through the esoteric teachings and practices of all peoples and eras. Indeed, human self-knowledge and self-realization ultimately derive all their meaning from it.*
Potentially, it is also the deepest source of understanding between the peoples, and can foster a further process, in which the unity that connects us all in true nature is fulfilled in the order and *wholeness of a universal human community*.

THE SHADOW

Our instinctive reactions on meeting something "different"—whether we reject it sharply (as if warding off a threat) or are strangely drawn to it—can open our eyes to the wholeness within us. Either way, we are actually reacting to a side of ourselves that our "normal" nature represses and overshadows, but that wants to be let in. In this sense, the Eastern often turns out to be the *shadow* of the Western. The vehemence that champions of the Western way often show in discussing the outlook of the East is usually a sign that the person concerned has met his or her *shadow*. This "shadow" is an unacknowledged part of that person's total self, and is clamoring to reach the light. If it is rejected, the person remains incomplete, "unwhole" in a way that inevitably provokes a crisis, and ultimately leads to sickness. It is essential to rec-

* Cf. René Guénon, e.g., *Le symbolisme de la croix* (Paris: Les Editions Vega, 1957); *Aperçus sur l'initiation* (Paris: Les éditions traditionelles, 1953).

ognize, accept, and integrate the shadow. This is why the Westerner must, to remain or become whole and healthy, learn to recognize, admit, and integrate his or her insufficiently acknowledged and repressed "Eastern" side.

When we say that Westerners have an Eastern shadow, what do we really mean? Are we thinking of specifically Eastern customs and traditions, of particular aspects of Eastern culture? Certainly not! We are thinking of certain *basic spiritual principles* that are not inherently "Eastern"—although racial and geographical conditions have made them more pronounced in the East than the West—and that are universally valid for human beings and essential to human wholeness. As primal possibilities, energies, and orientations on the path to selfhood, they belong to the basic texture of human life, although they are realized to differing degrees at different times and in different places. And since they are the basic themes of our humanity, they always involve religious problems as well. They are the existential roots of spiritual growth and change, which originate in life's deepest meaning and return to it. They are the archetypal shaping and developing principles behind every human process of becoming and coming to consciousness. They are within us from the start, but emerge to a greater or lesser degree depending on our life's circumstances. Stage by stage and in different ways, they also determine the special features of a people's development, way of life, and culture. And so the contrasting religious visions of East and West can serve not simply to distinguish peoples and regions, but to make us *ask* how the two were originally joined in human wholeness, and how they can be joined again in both East and West to make Easterners and Westerners whole to the benefit of everyone. Here, we can usefully start by considering the difference between the energies that have historically shaped the spiritual development of East and West.

THE EASTERN AND THE WESTERN SPIRIT

The culture of the West is essentially rooted in *knowledge* derived from the natural *experience* of our five senses and reflection on that experience, and in *belief* derived from divine revelation. Thus Westerners owe much of what they are today to science and its offshoot, technology, and to the Christian religion. In the East, however, the notion of a personal God has never had the importance it has always had in the Judeo-Christian-Islamic West, and reason has never been credited with power to resolve life's fundamental problems. Instead, the East has sought meaning and a solution to those problems in a third element—*supernatural experience* transcending natural consciousness ("natural revelation" might be another name for it). All the religious feeling and wisdom of the East center on the watershed *experience of otherworldly Life*, which has nothing to do with any worldly experience, and allows people to sense the possibility of escaping from the anguish caused them by the world-bound ego. The East's initiatory practices are all based on seeing this experience clearly as our starting point, way, and destination. Historically, the concept of initiation has always been more important to Easterners than Westerners—but it is, essentially, neither Eastern nor Western. From the mysteries of classical antiquity, through the Knights Templar, the Rosicrucians, the Freemasons, and even the alchemists, to their various counterparts today, the West has always had its esoteric circles, for whom initiation and transformation were key concepts. Admittedly, initiation has never been in the West what it is in the East—the remote and radiant destination on a way that all believers can travel. Instead, official religion and theology, and later the scientific spirit, have thrust it into the shadows. But the inner Way is essentially no more of an Eastern prerogative than the experience of Being, on which it is based—although it has always been more at home in the Eastern spiritual tradition. There are many reasons for this. For one thing, the Way of initiation, which begins and ends with the mighty experience of *unity*, accords with the Eastern character, while the dualism typical of Western religion (which emphasizes the ego and "contrasts" it with the world and with God) is more in tune with the Western mentality. This difference remains when the West takes over the notion of initiation. In initiation practice, East and West instinctively emphasize different aspects of the experience of Being. The differences are not simply the result of different religious traditions, but reflect differences in character and feeling for life. It is significant, for example, that there were no words in Japanese for "personality" or "work" (in the sense of a thing made by a specific person) until Western philosophy was studied in Japan. The notion of the self-contained artifact, with its own value and form, was simply not a meaningful one. Instead of tangible, *static form*, the Eastern life instinct and consciousness focus on *fluid form*—the flowing, featureless, fleeting All-One, which dissolves all form; instead of the self-shielding ego, the egoless losing of the self in the Absolute, and so on. Inevitably, the difference reappears in the placing of emphases in initiatory experience and guidance. And it also appears in the dominant conceptions of the Absolute—that is, in general religious feeling and in particular religions.

RELIGIOUS FEELING, EAST AND WEST*

If we look briefly at some of the basic differences between religious feeling in East and West, we find:

In the East, the *starting point* of all religious thought, feeling, and action is the concept of the "All-One," which we ourselves basically are. The starting point in the West is belief in God, the all-powerful Creator, on whom we depend and from whom we are utterly, permanently separated. The *goal* in the East is union with the All-One (beyond life and death, being and non-being); in the West, it is communion with God, with whom we never merge, but who comes home to us in faith as the mighty "You," from whom we are always distinct. In considering the differences, we must always remember that each of the two "standpoints" has both higher forms and lower ones—and be careful not to assume that our own form is always the highest, and the other side's the lowest. An Easterner, for example, makes this mistake by envisaging experience of the All-One as supra-antithetical consciousness, the product of a lengthy process of practice and maturing, and contrasting it with the most primitive form of natural consciousness, with its ego-world and ego-deity. A Westerner does likewise by taking the highest form of belief in God through Christ and contrasting it with a merely prepersonal sense of universal unity.

The Eastern Way leads the believer through a lengthy process of change away from individuation and the here and now to the experience of union with Being that cannot, ultimately, be experienced personally; the Western (Christian) Way, on the other hand, leads him or her through a process of individuation to a state of independent personhood, in

---

* Cf. A. Cutat: *La rencontre des religions* (Paris: Aubier, 1957).

which he or she assumes full responsibility for his or her own self. The East aims, in the encounter with the Absolute, at progressive dissolution of its "otherness" (with which it is familiar, but which it traces back to the divisive ego). Spiritual development in the West, on the other hand, aims at progressive revelation of this otherness—a process in which both the ego and true nature's individuality are fully brought out, affirmed, and acknowledged, and that culminates in free confrontation of the human and the divine persons, the ego in its highest form and the divine "you." Progressive depersonalization of both the seeker and the Absolute in the East contrasts with progressive personalization of both in the Christian quest.

Ultimately, the East is focused on nonpersonal Being, the West on a personal God. Ultimately, the only thing accepted as "real" by Eastern "knowledge" is the all-unity of Being, which resolves all distinctions and which rational consciousness conceals by seeing division everywhere and disregarding the fundamental oneness of things. The East also stresses that Being's own nature cannot be discussed, since experience of it cannot logically be compared with anything else. In Christian belief, the human and the divine remain separate, even when love of God brings the sense of an intimate bond between the two, or the mystical experience of unity seems temporarily to bridge the divide. Moreover, for Christians, human understanding is not something that generates an illusory multiplicity and conceals true nature's undivided unity, but something that shows us a genuine, God-created multiplicity, and allows us to perceive the divine in various forms and on various levels. At the same time, the child-father image that is used to convey the nature of the Christian's relationship with God is not really that of a relationship in which ego and transcendent deity are entirely separated.

The Eastern conception of reality ultimately dismisses the particular, the individual, the autonomous—and thus the I-You relationship derived from those notions—as an illusion. The ways of living and thinking that are constantly renewing and stubbornly protecting themselves in this illusion are seen as the outer signs of a consciousness that is certainly part of the human condition, but limited and the source of all suffering. This consciousness is grounded in the unreality of an ego that generates all error by first fragmenting the One and then clinging to the fragments. The doctrine of a consciousness that conceals Being is not "believed," but experienced on the deepest level. The proof that this experience is valid, and is being interpreted correctly, lies in the *illumination* that it brings, redeeming and freeing the sufferer in an instant from the anguish caused by these illusions. From a Western standpoint, this doctrine itself seems an illusion, or at least a fatal disregarding of the genuine fullness of existence that, far from detracting from divine Being, manifests it creatively. As time goes on, however, we find these blunt comparisons increasingly uncomfortable. Surely the East affirms the world's multiplicity as well? And is the notion of an illusion-spinning consciousness really something inherently Eastern—and not perhaps an insight of universal significance, to which the East has simply paid more attention?

YIN AND YANG

If we compare the conceptions of reality and the religious instincts of East and West in this way, the positions are clearly incompatible. In fact, positions and standpoints are always incompatible, since two things can never occupy the same ground simultaneously. Similarly, two opposite movements cannot coincide in space and time—any more than breathing out and breathing in. But what if the relationship between East and West were really the same as that between *breathing out* and *breathing in?* Breathing out and breathing in are dialectical poles in the breather's life-rhythm. In this sense, everything that lives is something that breathes, although those who have studied human beings, and indeed breathing, have said too little about this.

Breathing out and breathing in make sense only in terms of each other—and of the breather. Perhaps, indeed, the earth should be thought of spiritually as a mighty breathing process. Surely it might be seen, entire and in all its constituents, as breathing, living itself out, developing and driving toward an ever higher, ever subtler wholeness in the polar movement of two life impulses, a polar movement that is reflected in the relationship of Eastern to Western spirit, just as the relationship of male and female is reflected in every human being. This image, I believe, is a fruitful one—and indeed not simply an image.

The supreme breathing process! In it, the Far East sees, senses, and experiences absolute reality as *Tao.* With Tao as starting point and destination, the two poles between which Life oscillates are known as *yin* and *yang.* Western thought is now starting to incorporate the vital yin/yang polarity in its conception of the human. In doing so, it is not simply admitting the central element of Eastern wisdom, but is also opening itself to the fructifying influence of one of the basic principles that underlie any valid view of life.

What do we mean by yin and yang? We mean the convergence and coexistence of two primal principles, in which the whole of life embodies, disembodies, and reembodies itself in its own vital forms as they enter and pass out of being. Every form that exists is generated and impelled to distinct and complete realization of itself by Life. Every movement toward form is balanced, however, by a countermovement back to the All-One, which contradicts all individuation and fixation of form and draws them home into itself. And so every advance into the *particular* is matched by a retreat into the *unity* that dissolves it. In human beings, this movement appears in the interplay of male and female, paternal and maternal, heaven and earth, begetting and conceiving, creative activity and redemptive inactivity, willing and accepting, bright ego-world consciousness and dark unconsciousness, world-ego and God-infused true nature. But human *life* is always both at once. One without the other is neither yin nor yang. It is only in the circle that encloses both that the sign becomes valid and reveals its meaning fruitfully. Every living creature is the product of yin *and* yang, heaven *and* earth. This includes human beings, but human beings live fully only when they consciously follow the great law—that is, the *yin/yang rhythm*.

Breathing exists as a genuinely living process only in the interplay of breathing out that culminates in breathing in, and breathing in that culminates in breathing out. Pausing of the movement on one side or the other shows that life is losing its balance or is off-balance already; and whenever the movement stops, life ceases! This is why Life's "enemy" can be seen as operating in two ways: either arresting the process at the point where seemingly perfect form is achieved, holding fast to that form and narrowing it down to something fixed, the result being *paralysis*—or checking it at the point where form passes out of being and the movement toward new form begins, the result being *dissolution*. In either case, *tension* toward form and *relaxation* in the unity that absorbs and regenerates form lose their vital "simultaneity," and the deathly antithesis of *strain* and *dissolution* takes over. The first danger threatens the West, and the second the East. In both cases, Life stops breathing, and this means death.

In opening itself to the mystery of breathing, the West is not simply opening itself to one of the fundamental elements in practical Eastern wisdom, but also to the central, vitalizing source of our humanity. "Breath" is one of the basic principles of life. In breath, coming into being and ceasing to be, starting and finishing, the emergence and reabsorption of form, the appearance and disappearance of all existing things in the ground of Being are fulfilled and unfold in an everlasting cycle.* There are differences, however, between epochs, individuals, and also East and West in the placing of the emphasis—on "ceasing to be and going home" or on "coming into being and setting out." Easterners tend to focus on everlasting return, Westerners on everlasting departure. But although these differing emphases reflect differences in feeling for life and basic intention, human life is fruitful and complete only when it contains both elements. Similarly, the active and passive approaches to life must converge and coexist. Today, it is generally recognized that the West is overactive, and needs to grasp what "doing nothing" really means. It must learn to appreciate and accept those meditative practices that are, as initiation exercises, an essential part of traditional life-guidance in the East.

Of course, meditation has also played a central role in the life of our spiritual orders in the West, and still does so today. Particularly in the form of exercises (Ignatius of Loyola) and of prayer that takes us from "seeing" to "contemplating," it has been decisive in the teaching of such great mystics as van Ruysbroeck, Saint John of the Cross, and Saint Theresa

* Cf. Dürckheim: "The Practice of Breathing" in *Hara, the Vital Centre of Man*, translated by Sylvia-Monica von Kospoth and Estelle Healey (London: Unwin Paperbacks, 1977).

of Avila. They have not, it is true, shaped the Western way of life in any general sense. But if we today decide that we need to give meditation its proper place in our lives, we are not opting for something merely Eastern that contradicts our Western attitudes. What we are really doing is admitting that our ways of living in the West, which are largely determined by a frenzied pressure to produce, are incomplete and need something else as well. Introducing meditation is a part of making the West whole again, and becomes essential as soon as we accept the concept of initiation.*

The difference between religious feeling that starts and ends with experience of the All-One, and religious feeling that originates and fullfils itself in confrontation of the human "I" and the divine "You," is paralleled in the primal situations of early childhood. Babies are still wholly embedded in Being—there is a sense in which, even after birth, they are "still" in their mother's body—and something of this stays with us all our lives. This sense of being at home in the Great Mother, in the all-resolving, all-redeeming Absolute, remains permanently with us as one of our longings, and one of the directions our process of becoming can take. We only become fully human, however, when we start relating to a "you," when that "you" addresses us and we answer it.

Human beings are made for dialogue. It is therefore worth considering whether the I-You relationship's only purpose is to make us aware of the unity it threatens as it develops and sets firm—or whether it is not the intended expression of our own primal unity. Life grounded in the Absolute first expresses itself in the I-You relationship, but that relationship itself remains vital only while it is transcended by a reconciling whole, in which it repeatedly dies and is reborn.

As soon as we leave the vital *alternation* of primal unity

* Cf. p. 140 ff.

and I-You behind, adopt a fixed ego-stance and use it to locate and define our experience, "you" becomes "it." And since this "it" becomes real only by separating from the "I" and shedding all traces of it, it subverts the unity that exists between undivided "I" and personally experienced "you." Every "you" falls prey to this process (which typifies rational consciousness) as soon as we start to take an interest in its "objective" reality. It becomes an object, and must be stripped of all "subjective" elements. When we surrender to objectivization in this way, personal encounter becomes an impossibility, and God himself is ultimately pushed away and treated as a "thing." At this point, vital unity is utterly lost, and with it the divine presence, which can only be "encountered."

When we consider how the experiences of unity and dialogue relate, we may find ourselves asking: which is more important? The Eastern and the Western elements in our makeup part company on the answer. The East says unity; the West says dialogue! But surely both ultimately belong together? We can miss ourselves both by submerging completely in Being's primal matrix, and by leaving that matrix utterly behind. In fact, losing this close, basic contact with Being is an unavoidable part of our human condition and, when this happens, death—the "wages of differentiation"—enters our life. Restoring the link with Life beyond life and death is the purpose of all initiatory practice, and the first stage is always to sink fresh roots in the "mother-ground" of Being. But even in therapy, which is chiefly concerned with people who have lost their wholeness in a one-sided world of rational order, returning to the "maternal sphere" within us is decisive.

The "East/West" issue acquires special resonance once we start to consider how true nature and personhood relate.

TRUE NATURE AND PERSONHOOD

If true nature is the mode in which divine Being is present in us, then it also makes us part of a universal unity. In it, we *are* the All-One in our own individuality's language—and, *as* the All-One, we are also connected with everything else. We can thus say that we penetrate our true nature in the deepest sense only when (in our own individual manner) we admit the All-One so completely that we lose ourselves utterly in it. At this point, the "true self" (e.g., for the Hindu) is nothing but the All-One, and thus identical for all human beings—indeed all true natures. In true nature, we *are* the All-One, and coincide with all true natures. This is the Eastern view. We can also say, however, that the All-One manifests itself as it really is in the individual, unique true nature of every one of us. We thus find the way to our true selves only by finding the way to our individuality and releasing both it and, in it, the All-One in ourselves. And so Life commands us, not to dissolve individuality in the All-One, but to realize individuality in the "person." This is the Western view—that each of us can realize and manifest his or her share in all-uniting Being only by affirming his or her uniqueness in his or her own way. United in true nature and Being, divided in their ways of embodying and manifesting the Absolute—plants, animals, and humans all conform to this pattern. In humans, however, there is something else, something that raises them above all other creatures and takes the solitude out of individuality—the personal element in human consciousness. It is this that allows us, as individuals, to "encounter" others as individuals, in a way that engenders a special sense of community.

The whole question of personal encounter needs special consideration once we start thinking about the relationship between Eastern and Western spirituality. In both the Easterner's general feeling for life and specifically religious instincts, the concept of the person does not have the significance we give it in the West. This is also one of the main reasons why Westerners often feel they have nothing to gain by exploring Eastern attitudes and absorbing Eastern spiritual values.

I myself have studied the question of "personhood" in Japan, where the kind of encounter in which two people genuinely meet is unusual. Of course, there are outstanding, striking people in the East, as there are in the West—meeting a Japanese master is enough to make this plain. But is such a master a person in our sense of the term, or merely an exceptionally impressive personality?

People in Japan treat one another with the greatest respect, but what is the real basis of that respect? On the one hand, there is an unmistakable lack of compassion for suffering (including human suffering outside a person's family); on the other, there is profound respect for others in their suprapersonal true nature—otherwise, what or whom are the Japanese saluting in the deep, reverential bows that they often exchange on meeting?

I remember an old master, who had charge of a camp for young men selected to colonize Manchuria—robust, often rather coarse-looking youths from peasant families. Simply walking with him round the camp, I had been struck by the way in which he returned the young men's greetings—sometimes hardly at all, and sometimes with special courtesy. One day, we were sitting at tea when one of the young men brought a message and, before leaving, bowed deeply before the old man. To my astonishment, he rose and bowed deeply in return. When we were alone, I asked him, "Who were you bowing to just then—surely not the young man?" He looked at me and said, "No, of course not. To the point in him that is also in me!" And he added softly, "Tenno."* He himself was a Shintoist. Had he been a Buddhist, he would have said, "Before the Buddha-nature in him that is also in me"; as a Christian, he might have said, "Before Christ in him, who is also in me." But this "point" in others that is also in me—is it the person? No. Do I encounter the person when I perceive another human being's individuality and respond to it? Even then, the answer is still no.

Attaining personhood depends on a fusing of All-One, individual true nature, and world-ego that permits direct, immediate, and genuine manifestation of a freedom born only of contact with the Absolute, which is present in both true nature and world-ego. But this contact makes us persons in the full sense only when it frees us from the world-ego's shackles *and* also bears the mark of our individuality, experienced as something that we must realize. There is, however, a preliminary stage.

How does a Zen master know that a student has "made it," has had satori? He knows when the student suddenly appears before him for the first time in the fullness and power of true selfhood, simultaneously embodying what he or she is in true nature and what he or she has become in the world, uniting world-ego and true nature. Charged with an energy and radiance that point to presence *from* the Absolute, he or she comes to the master in full awareness of having been freed from the puny ego's clutches—daring at last, as it were, to be fully *himself* or *herself*. To a certain extent, he or she has already become a person. But this is where East and West part company. For the Eastern master, birth of the person from the union of world-ego and true nature is merely a *sign* that the student has tasted Being, and been freed in a general

* In Shintoism, the divine unifying principle, supremely incarnate in the Emperor.

sense from the world-ego's agonizing spell by the experience (although further exercise and change are needed to make this "redemption" an integral part of his or her essential nature). The individual form acquired in the process is not taken seriously as such, and so remains incompletely real. This, however, is the very thing that counts for Western masters: liberation from the superficial, world-bound, more or less functionalized and stereotyped ego frees the student *to become* the person that he or she individually is. For us in the West, it is more important that a new worldly form should emerge *from* true nature and witness to Being, which reveals itself in the world's rich multiplicity, than that the world-ego should dissolve *in* true nature and *in* Being, which is present in true nature. It is not the redemptive, but the creative act of Being (or aspect of the experience of Being) that we stress—generation of the person by the form-giving "Word." There is something else here that distinguishes West from East: we do not simply affirm fully realized individuality, but fully realized integration of true nature and *world-ego*—in other words, absorption of the Absolute into the *here-and-now body*.

It is this acceptance and sanctification of the here-and-now body—affirmed as something that reveals and mediates the divine self, and not as something that contradicts it—that first allows the person in the fullest sense to emerge. This may well be something specifically Christian. I remember once feeling a sudden urge to ask a Japanese woman who was temporarily working with me, "Mrs. Toda, are you a Christian?" "Yes," she answered in surprise. "How did you know?" My own response was unexpected for both of us: "Because your eye is so open!" In fact, it is typical of the Japanese that one rarely sees the "personal eye," rarely sees the individual as a particular person. He or she always appears in a specific role, as son, student, teacher, guest, Japanese, and so on. As master, he or she appears in a supreme form in which every personal element has been converted into something supra-personal, almost remote from the world, or at least not involved in it. One rarely, if ever, meets the happy or suffering individual, through whose joy-filled, sorrow-filled eye the otherworldly glimmers in a unique personal sense. I am not suggesting, of course, that every Christian has an "open eye"—this kind of presence is something that Christians have to work for too. I am merely pointing out that a personalizing principle is at work in Christianity—a principle that I have not encountered in that form in the East.

THE "DANGER" FROM THE EAST?

The Westerners who distrust Eastern religious feeling fall into two categories: those who champion Western attitudes in a general sense, and those who specifically champion Christian belief. The first attitude clearly expresses the shadow—one-sided emphasis of humanity's yang aspect and repression of its yin aspect. Of course, the shadow is undoubtedly present as well in the skeptical, hostile reactions of certain representatives of the Christian churches to everything Eastern (the form assumed by the church-based Christian religion is in fact more yang- than yin-determined). But Westerners are also wary of initiation practice for very specific reasons. Three main dangers are commonly mentioned here: *self-redemption, depersonalization* and *overemphasizing of the body*.

1. *Self-redemption*: Many Christians see a danger of illicit self-redemption as soon as people start thinking that exercise

can bring them nearer to God. Simply concentrating on one's own inner life seems to contradict a movement in which one attempts to focus on God as something unequivocally outside oneself. Thus Christian prayer, which involves giving God one's whole attention, steadily deepening one's concentration on Him, and tirelessly trying to discern His will, is contrasted with the effort to "master" one's own soul, which is ultimately seen as self-centered and dangerous. Of course, there are differences here—different "standpoints" in the religious process of becoming—but do they necessarily exclude one another? To answer this question, we must first take a careful, understanding look at what each side actually means and experiences. When the Japanese make a distinction between *tariki* and *jiriki* (literally autoredemption and redemption from outside), they mean that some people have not yet experienced the Absolute personally, and must therefore rely entirely on Amida-Buddha's saving mercy, while others must learn to recognize consciously and realize in their hearts that "salvation of the soul in Being" that has been there from the start, and has never not been there. This mystery can be *experienced* only in the otherworldly life of the soul, and experiencing it then becomes the objective of exercise. But this is not to say that to exercise is to "redeem oneself." What does redemption really mean? Here too, misunderstandings are frequent. To a Christian, redemption means redemption from sin and guilt—and both of these concepts are largely alien to the Eastern religious outlook. Redemption in the Eastern sense is redemption from suffering, and specifically the suffering caused us by the space-time world, and rooted in a consciousness that separates us from Being, but can be left behind. Being is beyond life and death, beyond all the dualities that torment us. To find it, we must expand our consciousness, and this allows us to overcome the world. Must this insight remain an Eastern privilege? To us it seems universally valid and significant. But is the Being we experience in this way God? Put in these terms, the question is too crass, for the experience of Being lies beyond the reach of "what-is-that?" inquiry. Anyone who asks where God is for people who have all-liberating experiences of Being without thinking specifically of God or Christ is best answered with another question: is there any reason why God should not speak to us *from* our deepest experiences? As a rule, these experiences actually prepare the ground for renewed belief in God when rationalization of the intellect has dried out the original soil by robbing us of personal contact with the divine.

2. *Depersonalization*: To reassure people who fear depersonalization in initiation exercise, we must first distinguish the puny, anxious, thing-fixated ego, which must be overcome (even when it is ethically admirable), from the emergent *person*, or new self, which cannot appear until that ego vanishes. Many Christians distrust and reject the exercises that neutralize the ego because they are afraid that God may be neutralized with it. This is why they insist on the need to stay permanently focused on God or Christ, never turning away for an instant. But this is a requirement that actually puts the whole process of attaining personhood at risk. It prevents the person performing the exercise from sinking trustingly into the supra-objective matrix, in which alone the ego, with its petrified image of God, can disappear, the true personal center open, and he or she can hear the divine call that is something more than the frightened, frustrated world-ego's echo.*

3. *Overemphasizing of the body*: It is strange that the East, whose religious instincts lead almost universally to discarding of the body, should make physical exercise (yoga) a natural part of inner change, while Christianity, for which the Word's becoming flesh is a central belief, exercises the body chiefly

* Cf. J. B. Lotz: *Meditation im Alltag* (Frankfurt/M.: Knecht, 1966).

to subdue its "materiality" and concomitant "sensuality." Obviously, a great deal of this is now being rethought, but it will still be some time before we stop rejecting the body and start recognizing the importance of transforming it so that the person can emerge.

The body's importance for the inner Way cannot be overestimated.* When we exercise, for example, we must learn to give ourselves to the rhythm of breathing, in which Life reveals itself to us, so completely that we really experience in it the fading and yielding of consummated form to new form, and the repeated emergence of form from formlessness—and so gradually generate the secure permeability in which the everlasting process of change can continue unchecked. And when the puny ego passes out of being, its God undoubtedly vanishes with it.

As the heirs of the Western Christian tradition, we must stop being afraid of forfeiting personhood if we let ourselves sink into the mother-ground of Being, and of betraying our beliefs if we open ourselves to the initiatory dimension. It is only when perfected personal form is repeatedly melted down in the crucible of the inchoate that a new person can repeatedly be born. Indeed "personhood" itself exists only as the movement of ever-creative, ever-redemptive Being—manifesting itself in us, and experienced, willed, and shared in by us at an ultimate point of heightened consciousness.

* Cf. Dürckheim: "Die Bedeutung des Leibes in der Psychotherapie," in Zacharias, *Festschrift für W. Bitter* (Stuttgart: Klett, 1968), and *Hara, the Vital Centre of Man*, loc. cit.

THE EXPERIENCE OF BEING AND BELIEF

The contradiction between experience-based religious feeling and Christian belief disappears once spiritual guidance starts to focus on otherworldly Being and on serving it. Once we accept the ongoing birth of form from Being and stop *wanting* final fusion with it, every return to the everlasting matrix automatically leads to a new setting out toward a new level of personhood, and the Absolute's personal form is itself repeatedly renewed. If, on this level, we repeatedly throw off the shackles of the world-dependent ego and here-and-now body, our *entire* "personhood" becomes, from the ego's standpoint, increasingly *suprapersonal*. Whenever we realize a new form of personal being in the yang's upswing, we must have the courage at once to throw everything we are, have, and believe into the yin's downswing. Again and again, we must dare to surrender all the hardened products of imagistic consciousness to those impenetrable depths in which images and forms fade and disappear, and in which, as Meister Eckhart puts it, "no Peter and no Paul" are left either. But we can rely on being repeatedly lifted from those depths and carried into a new form of personhood—a higher human stage that is free and responsible because it is ever more a part of otherworldly Life.

It is precisely those who have lost their beliefs who can find new access to belief in deepening contact with the Absolute, as they step out on the Way of initiation. They must simply learn to trust their deepest experiences, accept them as important, build on them, recognize their significance, and, taking them as a starting point, consciously practice surrendering to the process of change they initiate. Those who have the courage to sink utterly into the mother-ground of Being, remain there patiently, leave everything behind, and "trust the trip," can experience rebirth and—in Christian terms—the dawning of that sonhood or likeness to Christ, which constitutes their true nature (in which they are focused on Christ).

And so the "East/West" in ourselves also applies to religion. Of course, there is still a difference between "religion" based on the experience of Being and religion rooted in belief, and between religion that begins and ends in the impersonal All-One, and religion that begins and ends with a personal God. But experiencing Being does not simply mean experiencing the redemptive All-One—it also means encountering something that "calls" us and our own personal center. Conversely, *living* belief in a personal God includes the obligation of repeatedly melting down all our fixed images of God in the spirit and truth that transcend all images. Fundamentally, experience of suprapersonal Being and personal belief are not two different things, but parts of the same process. In live religious feeling, they start separate, and grow back together. It is only "religions" that divide. Live religious feeling unites—provided we retain our grip on the golden thread that is given to all of us as a redeeming, mandatory link with the Absolute.

A few words on the Absolute's "personality." Because we are human, and while we experience as ego-subjects, we experience everything as having a "face," and "determine" it from the world-ego. This is why we also picture the otherworldly Life revealed to us in our deepest experience as a personal being—even when we "theoretically" remain faithful to the impersonal All-One—and why our image of the central element in that experience is always a personal one. Like all the traditional elements that are handed down and live on as "inner" knowledge in initiates, this image comes to form part of a system of objectively determined beliefs and sets firm in an anti-Life manner if we see ourselves only in terms of world-ego consciousness, and make that consciousness our permanent home.

Any belief that is systematized in this way is in constant danger of petrifying with the concepts and images that embody it. To remain vital, all of this must be melted down repeatedly in that absolute reality that is *change* and itself transcends all images.

It is only in the oscillation between a personal and a nonpersonal pole that homo religiosus progresses. The movement that trustingly surrenders established belief to the fathomless process of otherworldly Life obeys Life's law by then swinging over to the converse movement, in which the supreme dissolving element itself reemerges as divine form. We must learn to see the basic process as one that redeems from form and also creates it. It is only because the East tends to present the ground of Being in its yin aspect only, and because the initiation process has so far reached us mainly in its Eastern mode, that it seems to us so completely incompatible with our Western instincts, and particularly belief in a personal God. In itself, the initiatory dimension is focused on neither yin nor yang, but on supra-antithetical Life—in other words, on Tao, the primal Life-rhythm, which lives itself out in yin and yang, and with which every religion (including Christianity) lives or dies.

In the West, we easily make the mistake of seeing the All-One as fundamentally nonpersonal, and contrasting it with the personal—but it lies beyond that antithesis too. In the initiation process, yin must be lived as well as yang, and each must swing over and become its opposite. The only difference between the Eastern and Western elements in ourselves and in the world lies in the placing of the emphasis. Westerners naturally emphasize yang, and feel that their religion of a personal God can understand Eastern religious feeling and incorporate it—but not vice versa.

When the initiatory dimension comes to the West, the emphasis will necessarily lie on the coming of personal life to form. But as soon as the West attempts to define its life-forms (including its religion's imagistic form) in any final sense, otherworldly Life will step in and teach it a lesson. The more obstinately the champions of the Western spirit cling to their positions, the more those positions will come under fire from the young, as Life uses their radicalism to ensure that its law of change is again respected. It is only by themselves becoming initiates that religion's chief spokesmen will learn to speak the universal language, and at last bear vocal witness to the initiatory stage in human development.

EXERCISE

To follow the Way of initiation is to follow a way of *practice*, a way that means exercise—tirelessly working on the self.

The first point to make here is that initiatory "work" is not something we "do," but something we *allow to happen*. It means listening, hearing, obeying, surrendering to a process, and admitting a new reality that touches us in ourselves and in everything around us, calling on us to change in a very special way, and impelling us to do so.

The Way starts and ends with attending to this *experience* and *allowing* the reality that lies beyond the normal one to operate. We must learn to pay heed when this new element touches us, to open ourselves to it and follow its summons, and we must be prepared to undergo the change that it demands of us. All of this is a part of setting out on the Way of initiation, but we can really enter that way only by breaking through the limitations of a conception that is actually a misconception of the self. To say it again, this misconception involves seeing ourselves and the world as "real" only to the extent that life can be known and mastered rationally. The time has now come for a radical change and for sober, realistic acceptance of those experiences in which a source of energy and meaning that surpasses our normal ego-world capacities reveals itself unmistakably, undeniably, unequivocally, and powerfully as our own real center and the world's true nature. We must learn to let these experiences happen, must increase our capacity for them through exercise, and must learn to travel the resulting way of change systematically—must open ourselves, in a word, to *practice*.

THE THREE ASPECTS

The Way of initiation is exercise aimed at revelation of Being in existence. It is exercise in this sense only when it serves Being utterly, and is free of all pragmatic side-intentions—particularly the world-ego's efforts to misuse the process to boost its own power. Working on the Way breaks down into three essential tasks:

1. Developing the sensitivity needed for contact with Being.
2. Gaining insight into the conditions on which the experience of Being depends.
3. Practicing to eliminate everything that separates us from Being and develop everything that connects us with it. The purpose of this is to achieve an overall state (including the body) that enables us to stay in touch with Being and manifest it in the world.

Putting it differently, our first task is to cultivate transcendent *experience*, and the emphasis this places on Being's
presence in true nature makes the Way's esoteric character
particularly clear. Our second task is to dismantle everything
(the unpurified subconscious, the shadow!) that prevents us
from experiencing Being and witnessing to it. This is the *depth-
psychological* part of the Way. Our third is to work systematically toward change (including physical change), and this
involves practice in the narrower sense—that *practice toward
wholeness* that includes the body.

We shall now look at each of these areas in greater
detail.

1. Our first task is to work tirelessly to develop and
refine the sensitivity needed for inner awareness of Being.*
Essentially, this means that we must practice perceiving and
attending to the specific qualities in which Being touches us
—either in ourselves or in the world. What we are learning
to do here is to detect the "wholly other," that is, the *numinous*.

"The outer is the inner exalted to a mystery," says
Novalis.** When this "inner" element touches us, the world
is utterly transformed. The kind of sensitivity necessary here
involves the whole person. We are open or closed to Being
in a total sense, which includes our consciousness of the present moment, of ourselves, and of the world around us. Somewhere deep within ourselves, we must be aligned on the
numinous, and must preserve a special alertness that ensures
that our "feeling" for the Absolute is constant. Developing
"transcendent memory" is a part of this, and manifests itself
in fidelity to past experiences of the Absolute, which cannot
be summoned up too often. These experiences are the golden

* Cf. H. Kükelhaus: *Werkstatt, Forum 8,* 1967.
** Novalis (Friedrich Leopold, Freiherr von Hardenberg, 1772–1801), poet and
early theorist of romanticism.

thread occasionally glimpsed in life's tapestry, and we must learn to see them not as exceptions or even mistakes in the weave—but as part of the true golden pattern that underlies the whole, and that our one-sided worldly fixations have stitched over and obscured. We must develop the special extrasensory sensitivity we need to perceive the absolute quality in relative phenomena, and to see this quality as expressing their real essence.

"It is by no means only the radiant, unforgettable turning points, whether terrible or joyful, in which Being comes home to us, and from which we live in a permanent sense. There are also the less striking moments and hours, when we suddenly find ourselves in a special state in which, without our understanding what is happening, Being touches us. Suddenly, without warning, we feel strange. We are wholly present, totally there—and yet not focused on anything definite. In a peculiar way, we feel 'round,' 'closed,' and yet opened, as a mighty inner fullness reveals itself. We seem to be floating, and yet move surely and steadily on the earth. We seem to be absent, and yet are totally present and filled with life. We rest wholly in ourselves, and yet are related to everything on the deepest level. We are raised above everything, and at the same time within everything—connected to everything and tied to nothing. We feel that we are being mysteriously led, and at the same time are free. We feel that we possess nothing and that nothing has a claim on us—that we are outwardly poor, and yet inwardly replete, powerful and rich. In moments like this, we feel that something very precious and also very fragile is working through us and within us. This, very probably, is why we move with unconscious caution, taking care not to stop and look too closely at what is happening to us."*

* Dürckheim: *The Way of Transformation: Daily Life as a Spiritual Exercise*, op. cit.

Our ability to have this kind of experience varies dramatically with the stage we have reached, our character, and our own past experience. Of course, although objective consciousness divides us from Being, ontological affinity ensures that we all have an inner longing to unite with it. This longing is naturally stronger in people who, perhaps without knowing it, have already had an exceptional experience in which Being has touched them. This may have happened at a crisis or turning point, or it may have taken the form of an intense childhood experience. Indeed, most adults carry the traces of such a childhood experience.

The Absolute is still reflected directly in the child's consciousness. Until the ego/world and ego/true nature divergence produces a final split, it remains present and operative in everything he or she experiences. This gives those experiences a special quality, and explains our nostalgia for childhood, as well as the lure of primitive peoples, who are still in touch with the other dimension.

Vivid experiences of Being are particularly common at that moment in childhood when, just as the ego is starting to assert itself, and objective consciousness beginning to develop, the Absolute suddenly wins through again as gladdening inner experience.

As long as we merely look back, childhood nostalgia is sterile and unhelpful. It can, however, become a fruitful starting point for conscious exercise if we can recapture the special quality remembered from childhood in our inner consciousness. Deep within ourselves, we can then understand what "becoming as little children" really means: to overcome separation from Being, which has always remained intact in our true nature, and allow union with it to become once again the dominant element in consciousness.

2. Exercising toward *insight* is a systematic realization and deepening of our knowledge of the conditions on which

the experience of Being depends. Three kinds of insight are involved: insight into the polarity of world-ego and true nature, insight into the shadow, and insight into the stages of human becoming, and particularly the transformation of consciousness.

a) Insight into the relationship of world-ego and true nature can come only from our own experience. As we exercise, we must *experience* in ourselves the difference between the contingent, world-focused subject-center (the world-ego) and our true nature's center, which is itself absolute and yet strives to manifest itself in the contingent. We must also experience the difference between the world-ego and the personal subject, which grows toward ever greater freedom from the fusion of world-ego and true nature.

b) We also need insight into everything that stands between us and our true nature, and prevents us from uniting with it, and becoming transparent in the process. This involves two things: recognition of the part that ego-world consciousness plays in preventing true nature from coming to consciousness, and insight into what we call the *shadow*—the sum total of our rejected (unlived or repressed) potentials, reactions, and impulses. The world-ego's "blocking" power is a result of the static character of the life systems it generates. These prevent "dynamic" true nature, whose element is unceasing change, from becoming effective. Moreover, the world-ego, with its will to possessions, prestige, and power, is constantly trying to displace true nature from the center, and this also interferes with the process of becoming.

To identify and understand the shadow, we need all the knowledge that modern depth-psychology has given us, and particularly its theory of repression—all of it bound to become increasingly a part of any educated person's intellectual equipment. But it is not enough to know about the shadow in theory. It is only by meeting it in practice—by discovering, acknowledging, and facing up to it in ourselves—that we can achieve that purification of the unconscious that is vital to sure progress on the inner Way.

c) Finally, we need insight into the various *stages in the inner process of becoming*. The following points are essential here:

When we start working on ourselves, we are already at the world-ego stage, and have already assumed a subjective form in which we leave primal unity behind and forge an independent personality.

The real "Way" begins, and the initiatory turning point is reached, when we break through that form's petrified concept, value, and behavior system. It is only by "transgressing" our normal reality in this way that we open ourselves to the other dimension. Taking the decisive step is always, too, a matter of having the courage to sink into the *mother-ground*, accept the mighty female principle in ourselves, and let it become effective. It is only when we admit the cosmic depths and sink into the *earth* that the *heaven* can open, the other-worldly spirit blaze through, and the *Logos* come to consciousness. It is only the union of heaven and earth that allows the *higher human being* to emerge. Initially, this higher human being remains wholly in the absolute sphere, beyond space and time—remote from the world, and so incompletely human. This is why we cannot really advance on the Way until we have understood the difference between experiencing the Absolute and changing in the way dictated by that experience.

Freeing us from the confines of our angst-ridden, cold, and somber world, our first genuine experiences of Being are registered primarily as redeeming light. But we are mistaken if we imagine that we can simply remain in that light, which actually arms us to encounter the darkness for the first time. Absolute light seems to summon absolute darkness—and it is only when we encounter absolute darkness that the real transformation can begin.

Invariably, the genuine experience of Being summons the "enemy"—usually some extraneous event that threatens to rob us of the benefit that our first joyful contact should bring us. At the same time, that first contact steels us to face the dark places in ourselves, and shows us the world's genuinely destructive capabilities for the first time. In short, it gives us the courage to look the dark forces in the face and encounter them bravely in reality. The way to transformation from true nature inevitably leads through this encounter—the encounter that first scalds us in the dragon's blood and enables us to witness to the otherworldly in the world. And it is the antithesis of absolute light and absolute darkness that first offers us the chance of ascending to that otherworldly sphere in which we leave antitheses behind and attain Light beyond light and darkness.

Gaining insight into these stages is not a matter of rational learning, but a harsh, step by step process of maturing, in which joy alternates with pain, and slow development with sudden breakthroughs.

3. The third aspect of work on the Way covers those exercises that aim directly at change, and affect our bodies too. The prerequisite here is a new conception of the body, which is no longer distinguished from soul and mind, but seen as the whole human being's bodily mode, or way of *being there*. Once we start aiming at transparency, transparency in the body becomes a particularly important part of it.

Normally, we notice our bodies only when they hurt or refuse to function, and cultivate them only for the purpose of increasing our physical stamina or improving our worldly performance. Once we start thinking in terms of the inner Way, however, we must listen to the body in a wholly different sense. We must learn to understand its "religious wisdom," that is, read the subtle signs that tell us how physical personality also relates to the Way, and how we are faring in those terms. But we cannot exercise toward this correctly without seeing the body itself correctly—and this chiefly means distinguishing the body we *have* from the body we *are* as personal subjects in the world.

"Exercising on the Way" is never a matter of toughening the body and keeping it healthy to gratify the worldly, self-asserting ego, but of changing our *personal* bodily mode. In this, we are guided by a special *body-conscience* that is geared not to health or good looks but to transparency. The bodily defects that it registers have nothing to do with sickness or deformity in a medical sense, but are obstacles to transparency—and they all have personal significance.

Seen in this way, hypertension thus appears as an attitude that contradicts true nature—and manifests the alienated, distrustful ego. This type of tension is aberrant, and constitutes a kind of frozen gesture, in which we cling to ourselves and, either defensively or aggressively, resist the world outside. To correct this tendency, we do not use technical "relaxation exercises," but simply allow gestures that express a basic confidence to substitute for gestures that express distrust of life. This is also the only way of releasing the ego-forces and allowing them to function correctly in the world. Seen in these terms, posture, tension, and breathing must not be regarded and assessed as parts of an overall functional mechanism, but as ways in which we reflect, express, and realize ourselves bodily as persons.*

In the West, initiatory work on the body is mostly familiar only in the form of "yoga," and hatha-yoga itself (whose intentions are "spiritual") is normally reduced to a form of gymnastics. Recently, the West has also started to take an

---

* The author discusses the bodily aspect of the inner Way in: *Hara, the Vital Centre of Man*, and in: *Sportliche Leistung-Menschliche Reife*, (Munich: Limpert, 2nd edition, 1967).

interest in Zen Buddhism, including both *zazen* (the basic exercise, seated meditation) and all the exercises that center on everyday actions. The best known of these is archery (cf. Eugen Herrigel, *Zen in the Art of Archery*; New York: Random House, 1971), and their basic purpose is to turn technical mastery into a mirror, and bring wrong inner attitudes to light in a never-ending process of repetition. There is nothing Eastern about exercising on this principle, and we do not need Eastern practices to apply it.

When we work toward "bodily rightness" of the whole person, we are always aiming at form that accords with true nature—the relaxed, opened form that is also a formed, relaxed openness to Being, and in which we are transparent, that is, capable of receiving Being and also capable of letting it operate through us in the world.

EXPANDING CONSCIOUSNESS

Expanding consciousness is one of the most important aspects of the Way of initiation.

The three aspects of initiatory "work" are all subsumed in the development of consciousness through various basic forms that reflect different modes and basic attitudes of the "subject." In his book *The Ever-Present Origin*, Jean Gebser has traced the development process from the magical through the mythical to the mental, and beyond it to integral consciousness, and has shown that each successive stage of consciousness not only builds on, but also—in a certain sense—contains all the earlier ones. The vital thing on the Way of initiation is to avoid regressing, and to progress to that "subjective" consciousness in which all the earlier stages, and particularly rational consciousness, are absorbed and transcended in a broadened consciousness.

When we say that the Way of initiation opens the door to otherworldly Life, we do not mean that unspecified higher faculties allow the old self to attain a higher sphere. What we mean is that we ourselves must become the door, must ourselves be remade. This implies total conversion: a 180 degree swing from the here-and-now *world* as center—with the otherworldly serving at best as prop, backdrop, or excuse for rejecting it—to the Absolute as center, with the old world serving to reveal it. To achieve this turnaround, we must be changed utterly—in mind, soul, and body. This is the only way in which otherworldly Life can open within us. But what does "open" mean? It means open *in consciousness*, or better, *as* consciousness.

We must become sufficiently transparent for Being to manifest itself in us as Life, consciously sensed, responsibly accepted, and pouring itself out into the world. To make this possible, our consciousness must change—not just our perceptive and affective consciousness, but also the bodily consciousness in which we register ourselves as "gesture." At the center of the new, otherworldly consciousness stands the subject, now identified with his or her *true nature*, whose coming to consciousness progressively rolls the horizons back on all sides—toward the otherworldly and cosmic, and also toward the "Logos." From now on, consciousness as *affective experience* is also dominated by the numinous. When we are transformed in the body, we become transparent in the body too.

It is only by becoming a *new person* that we can see *in a new way*, and only by seeing in a new way that we can see *new things*. As Goethe tells us in "Xenien," the eye cannot see the sun unless it has something of the sun in itself.

———

When we are really advancing on the Way—when we are increasingly entering the otherworldly and being absorbed by it as a *whole* person—we are transformed both in consciousness, *as* a subject who perceives and feels, and in the body, as a subject who acts.

As we have already said, the ontological basis for change is provided by our sharing in Being in our own true nature; our actual readiness to change, and the necessity of doing so, are both conditioned by our alienation from Being and the anguish it causes us. But this alienation is itself primarily due to the fact that our form of consciousness ("we" as conscious beings) is out of tune with Being to start with.

The consciousness that accords with Being is *deep*. By comparison, objective consciousness is too *shallow*, too *narrow*, and too frequently *static*. The purpose of initiatory "work" is to deepen and broaden ordinary consciousness, and to set things moving again in the process of change that true nature demands.

In modern therapy, too, the first stage is always to get the inner person moving again, to break through the shallow crust of ordinary consciousness to the individual and collective unconscious, and to realize the archetypal energies and images that underlie the process of becoming. Is this already the broadening of consciousness we seek on the Way of initiation? Not necessarily. For another, vital element is needed—*the otherworldly* must be present, together with an *all-pervading sense of the numinous*. All the steps we have listed may indicate that consciousness is being deepened, broadened, and galvanized in a merely quantitative sense, whereas we are concerned with a qualitative leap—the leap to the reality revealed in the numinous. It was C. G. Jung who taught us to perceive the numinous character of archetypes, and indeed to see the encounter with the numinous as an essential part of working on the self.

EXPERIENCING THE NUMINOUS

In his useful book on Indian wisdom and Western therapy,* Dr. Hans Jacobs starts one of his chapters by remarking: "There are two kinds of knowledge—rational knowledge, which is concerned with the transient, and spiritual knowledge, which is concerned with the eternal." How simple that sounds! For Indians, indeed, it is hardly worth saying, but we Westerners need someone to show us the difference between rational knowledge, which builds on sense experience, and the other, nonrational knowledge, which derives from extrasensory experience. This second kind of knowledge has a special numinous quality, and we must be able to perceive, recognize, and attend to it. We can make ourselves receptive to that quality by learning to do two things: to register and face up to a wholly new *element*, which can touch us at any time in any of the things around us, and to develop the other *form of consciousness* and accept it. The nature of the "new element" can be sensed directly in those experiences in which absolute fullness, form, and unity come home to us. But what is this other form of consciousness?

I once seized my chance to ask the old master, Daisetz Suzuki, about the difference between Eastern wisdom and Western knowledge, and immediately got the answer: "Western knowledge looks out, Eastern wisdom looks in." Smiling, he then added, "But if we look in as we look out, we end by turning 'in' into 'out.' " In other words, if we look at the inner sphere as if it were an object, we miss the very thing we are looking for in it—the supra-objective. The inner sphere in this case is the nonobjective, the otherworldly. The sin against the Holy Ghost is thus committed less by the puny ego, with its

---

* Cf. Jacobs: *Indische Weisheit, westliche Therapie* (Munich: J. F. Lehmann, 1966).

greed for pleasure, prestige, possessions, and power, than by that force in ourselves that pins us to objective consciousness and prevents us from rising above it.

One of the puzzling things about our development in the West is the way in which our spiritual leaders have avoided guiding us toward the higher realities that we can *experience*, and have obstinately restricted us instead to the lowest of all realities—those that objective consciousness can handle. Anything that cannot be known or mastered rationally has been declared a matter of faith and handed over to the theologians. This illustrates the immense power of opinion, be it theological or scientific, over direct experience. Opinion is the sole arbiter of what we are allowed to take seriously, and effectively prevents otherworldly, and indeed superhuman, experience from exerting its full force and winning through to acceptance. This, however, is where things are changing today. The first stage in that change is rejecting all fixities and giving the numinous our full attention as the harbinger of otherworldly Life.

Transparency as openness to the numinous, in which the Absolute reveals itself in special moods, qualities, and impulses, particularly means openness to those motive, mandatory, and transforming energies that enter us from the other dimension, make us over, and enable us to operate in a new way. When we have the right permeability, the Absolute determines and enters us with dynamic force. Sometimes it touches us as a gentle summons, imperceptibly drawing or pushing us on; sometimes it hits us like a thunderbolt, hurling us out of and beyond ourselves, or pitching us into unknown depths. But we can have various experiences of the numinous and still not register them properly or realize what they mean. This is why every system of practice must pay special attention to the moment when the seeker "experiences" this quality consciously for the first time—realizes fully that something new and unknown has just touched him or her.

Contacts with Being vary in intensity and duration, and must be distinguished from the experience of Being. People today—having first rejected the whole concept—now tend to speak of this experience too lightly, as if it was an everyday matter and familiar to everyone. But it is, and always will be, something rare and special—even for people who are in more or less permanent contact with the Absolute. And this is why the first priority should be simply making contact, rather than preparing for a possible future experience of the Absolute. Opinions differ as to whether the watershed experience itself is something unique, which transforms us once and for all, or something that can be repeated. Suzuki once said to me: "At the beginning of their spiritual development, some people have a small satori which shows them what the real issue is and launches them definitively on the great quest. It points the way, serves as a yardstick, and becomes a permanent part of their seeking and their working on themselves. When they later have genuine satori, this *experience* effects the great *change* as well. With other people, it's the other way round. They have no small satori at the beginning, and their seeking is rooted entirely in longing and in intuition. When the experience catches up with them, it's certainly tremendous—but a lot of hard work is still needed to achieve the transformation." The great master Hakuin* said of himself that he had had several great and many minor satoris. Generally, however, the "big" words, satori and samadhi,** are best avoided.

The "numinous" is the living heart of every religious experience. We have no proper word for it in everyday English. "Holy" is not entirely right since, although everything holy is undoubtedly numinous, not everything numinous is holy. The French use two concepts, *saint* and *sacré*, holy and

---

* Cf. Dürckheim: *Hara, the Vital Centre of Man*, a text by Master Hakuin.
** State of illumination and fusion resulting from contemplation of (not concentration on) an object.

sacred. The term "holy" is always used personally—of God or Christ as person, of the holy Mother of God, the Holy Spirit, and the saints. Turning away from traditional belief, and thus personal concepts of holiness, almost seems to have left people today with a general reluctance to accept the numinous and sacred. We must restore our natural relationship with the sacred. Indeed we must recognize that the sacred—and beyond it, the numinous—occupy the highest place in the hierarchy of qualities that we can experience.

"Numinous" is a broader concept than "sacred." It takes in the ambivalence, the darker sides of the Absolute. It is a quality that can be experienced in everything—in nature, other people, the dance, the erotic, and art (e.g., when the word "beautiful" is no longer enough). As R. Otto showed with the holy,* there is always something in it that both terrifies and fascinates us. Using C. G. Jung's word, it "overpowers" us, and lifts us, with a force that both exhilarates and frightens us, out of the world-ego's everyday sphere and into another dimension, destroying and liberating us at the same time. When it does this, it always carries us in some sense beyond ourselves. Particularly in the master's presence, this mysterious ambivalence is strongly felt wherever the traditional initiatory skills are followed in Japan—in the archer's gallery, the judoka's hall, and the rooms where ritual swordsmanship is practiced or the tea ceremony performed. There is danger in the air—the danger of perishing with the old ego; but for that very reason, the air is also charged with the promise of new being. This is why danger and promise are always associated with the Way of initiation, which is focused on the numinous.

The numinous, which incorporates the sacred, is the quality in which the Absolute touches us in a very general

* Cf. Rudolf Otto: *Das Heilige* (Munich: Beck, 1987).

sense. The holy touches us, however, only as the presence of personal Being. When *personal* fulfillment is the ultimate focus of our religious instinct, the holy and the sacred combine in an experience of Being *that has individual validity for us*. But *in* this experience, the person is surely nothing if not a medium for otherworldly true nature present in the experience itself.

The first stage in developing the sensitive consciousness needed for contact with the Absolute is learning to distinguish between objective consciousness, which divides, and "subjective" consciousness, which recognizes that subject and object are essentially one, and allows them to unite.* In this consciousness, we ourselves *are* to some extent what we "have" in it. Thus skilled craftsmen and artists are subjectively united with the *implements* they use and the *artifacts* they make, even though they remain objectively conscious of these as separate entities as well—especially when their *technique* is still not fully mastered. Their work is not complete and perfect, however, until all three are subjective presences only—and united in the person. In other words, perfection depends on their fusing with a technique that is totally mastered, and thus nonvolitional, and selflessly surrendering that technique to a deeper power that operates through them and achieves a flawless result without their doing anything.

A special kind of "listening within" and "being open from within" are vital to development of the right subjective consciousness. We must learn to tell defining consciousness, which resembles an *arrow*, from a consciousness that is totally open and receptive, does not define or judge, and resembles a *bowl*; in other words, *male* consciousness, which penetrates, seizes, analyzes, and "constructs," from *female* consciousness, which is essentially receptive, melts down and remakes what-

* Cf. Dürckheim: "Die transzendente Bedeutung der Ichwirklichkeit," in *Erlebnis und Wandlung* (Stuttgart/Berne: H. Huber, 1956).

ever it encounters, and releases it again as something new. Developing this female bowl-consciousness is the first stage on the Way of initiation. It marks the first step away from compulsive objective definition, and the first step toward presence of the Absolute in consciousness. The next stage is developing a consciousness in which we aspire toward Being in a total sense, seeking to make it an integral part of our own human wholeness. This consciousness is not located in the "head," but rather in the back of the neck or, more accurately, in the whole spinal column—and more accurately still, perhaps, in the whole body. This, at any rate, is how it feels. It affects and is sensed in everything we are as a kind of taut readiness to receive and surrender to the unknown—to "something in the air."

To develop the bowl-consciousness that frees us from the defining vision, and opens and prepares us for the absolute vision, we must practice *withdrawal*—an exercise vital to all progress on the Way. As long as we identify with the worldly ego, we are constantly sacrificing Being's nearness and our own transparency by objectively defining the things that preoccupy us at any given moment. When we do this, we are no longer present from true nature, but are wholly "focused" on the world and by the world-ego. Withdrawing puts us back in touch with our own true nature's depths, opens our inner eye and ear to the depths of the world's true nature, and shifts our attention from merely objective phenomena to "valencies," which the Absolute softly irradiates. This is why artists repeatedly distance themselves and stand back from their work, withdrawing from close, objective scrutiny into the broader inner vision that shows them whether the work itself is transparent. It is only people on whom the world has no hold who can see the Absolute through it.

Walking in the woods, we may stop for a moment, forget where we are going, and listen, without focusing on anything in particular, to the forest around us and the vast, mysterious stirrings of life within it. In the same way, we can—and must—learn to stand back in our daily lives and make room for absolute reality and depth in ordinary consciousness. This is a way of being in the otherworldly in the heart of worldly activity. The mature vision, which sees through the carapace of worldly form, comes from a faraway dimension. In the same way, serenity rooted in the Absolute communicates itself to other people too, and makes them permeable to the Absolute by allowing true nature to emerge and the world-fearing ego to fade out.

THE TRIUNITY OF BEING

Being touches us in three ways: as absolute *plenitude*, as *order*, and as *unity*, of which the human correlatives are *gladdening strength*, *feeling for form*, and *love*.

Initiatory living really begins only when we realize that our purpose in life is to serve the otherworldly in the world, and accept that mission. Just as reason's ultimate purpose is to clear the way for something that transcends it, so human beings are fully, successfully human only when they mediate the superhuman in everything they experience and do—and only to the extent that they do so.

When we are exercising toward perceiving Being in existence, we can choose to focus on one of its three primal aspects—fullness, form, and unity—for every experience has a quality that particularly evokes one of those aspects, and each of them has its own exercises. Of course, Being always touches us in everything we are, and there is no way of exercising toward it that does not involve the whole person. Indeed, the more total our involvement, the closer our experience comes to the Absolute.

Everything we are is reflected in everything we experience. There are no "isolated" sense impressions—they are always registered, and indeed determined, by the whole percipient. And so all of them—noise, music, a night bird's call, scents, pain—affect us in a total sense, touch the chords of our wholeness, and set them all vibrating.

But just as every such impression resonates through everything we are, so everything we are gives it its own special quality. We can get at the general through the particular, and we can similarly influence the fragmented components of experience by making changes at the center. Where practice and exercise are concerned, this means that the process is always two-way.

Attaining the right center is vital to progress on the way, and this is, first and foremost, a matter of constantly *renewing our basic commitment* to the Way, of *focusing on basic experiences* in which that commitment came home to us, and of *constantly practicing certain basic attitudes* that are essential to change.

When we practice tasting Being in existence, we are actually doing nothing new, but are simply bringing a quality that world-ego consciousness conceals from us to light. This absolute quality runs through the whole of our lives and experience like a secret thread and, when it surfaces in consciousness, it always has a special depth and breadth. It may come with shattering force, or as softly as breath. Always, however, it lifts us out of an impasse of which we had been only partially aware. It gives us a sudden sense of freedom, and in this freedom there are three elements—gift, promise, and summons. The gift is the fullness of Being, as it forces its way into us; the promise is the promise of a higher Life; and the summons is the summons to prepare ourselves for it. We must hear the summons, but hearing the summons depends on understanding the promise, and understanding the promise depends on Being's getting through to us—on our being open to it in a total sense. This is something toward which we can exercise.

THE NUMINOUS AND THE SENSES

It is chiefly through our *senses* that we perceive the *fullness* of Being. This is why initiatory practice involves, above all, cultivating the senses in a way that increasingly opens us to Being's presence by sharpening and refining our ability to detect the deeper dimension in all sense-qualities. "Cultivation of the senses as the intermediaries between above and below, inner and outer, is something that must be taken seriously all along the line" (Maria Hippius).

Reaching the point of exhaustion in our efforts to grasp and master life rationally leaves us spent and empty, but also ready to open ourselves once again to the miracle of the senses. The more concentration on surface phenomena makes our life shallow, and the more concentration on conceptual "mastery" of the world's multiplicity makes us lose sight of Being's fullness, starving our depths and causing us to suffer, the more sensitive we become to those moments in which something touches our true nature. At this point, we are also ready to rediscover the deeper dimension of the senses, and in it the wellspring of a Life that lifts us out of a shallow, devitalized existence that has lost all contact with the primal source.

Recognizing the senses as a source of transcendent experience has always been a basic feature of esoteric practice everywhere. Thus the inner meaning and symbolism of colors, the tonal impact and language of sounds, the power of scent to enter consciousness and alter it, the power of certain bodily movements to transform the whole person (yoga), the power of sexuality to lift us out of normal consciousness—all of these have always served as aids to transcendent experience, initiatory exercise, and personal change. Our task today is to take these insights over, eliminate their elitist character, and make them generally available to the growing number of people who have heard the call and whose innate developmental stage or individual destiny and maturity have brought them close to the point where the world-ego can and must surrender its hegemony, and they themselves begin to serve the Absolute consciously.

It is joy in living that first reveals absolute fullness to us ("I delight in living," said Meister Eckhart)—particularly when we experience it directly as bubbling root-energy, as maturing, effective, penetrating power, and as liberating warmth. Systematically bringing "standing and living in fullness" into consciousness is a part of initiatory exercise, and the only way of making the senses the gateway to the depths, so that Life can really open up in them: bathed in the glory of its radiant colors and sounds, constantly, surprisingly remade in the interplay of its forms small and great, full of tension and danger, but also and always full of promise. This radiant fullness of Being, experienced as burgeoning life, as an urge to be up and doing, as motive energy and dynamic force, as vitalizing breath, as corruscating, resounding, scenting, tasting, driving, impelling, warming, alluring, and liberating infinity—all of this comes to us through our senses.

Anyone whose heart is entirely or partly closed to this abundance is impoverished. But it is only by deepening our impressions, and never simply by multiplying them, that we open up the riches of Being.

Feeling Life through a deepened sensuality is one of the preconditions of genuine contact with Being. For just as normal sensuality provides a basis for development of the rational mind, so the emergence of a *suprasensual sensuality* is necessary to development of the spiritual mind. This exalted sensuality can develop only when the ordinary kind disappears.

There are exercises that center on "dying to the senses" and can help us to develop this new quality. There are also exercises in which we set out to create a void within ourselves and so banish the world's multiplicity, this being the only way of enabling Being's fullness to open. But before we can think about this kind of exercise, we must develop a new, extra-sensory feeling for Being's presence in normal sense experience. In seeing, hearing, tasting, smelling, and touching, in our overall bodily perception of ourselves, in erotic encounter—in all of this we can learn to sense and savor Being as "fullness."

Just as the gourmet (unlike the gourmand) ultimately finds in a classic wine a "savor" that no longer has anything to do with drinking in the ordinary sense, so all the senses have their own equivalents of "feeding," "eating," and "savoring," and follow the same progression until *prana* is reached, this being the Indian term for the vital, otherworldly energy in which the Absolute reveals itself in finespun material form through the senses.

And so there are various levels of sense perception. We must learn to distinguish the perceptive mode proper to the worldly ego and its natural capacities from all those experiences that go beyond—transcend—it. Listening to Mozart's music, we may find it "beautiful"—and suddenly there is something in it that leaves the word "beautiful" behind. Somehow, it goes "through and through" us, making us shiver with delight. This experience belongs to another dimension, "transcendent" both in depth and substance. The same thing can happen with pure sense experience.

Basically, all our experiences are either secular or transcendent, and we can work on developing the sensitivity we need to distinguish the two. We can understand all of this better by thinking of the variations in the way we ourselves are and feel at any given moment. For example:

We can feel vital or inert, energetic or lethargic, rich or poor, full or empty to varying degrees, and can feel all of this in both a secular and a transcendent sense. Being reveals itself throughout in the presence—or absence—of absolute fullness.

We can feel more or less "on-form"—centered, composed, right, adjusted, and "with it," or "off-form"—uncentered, tense, unfocused, rigid and "out of it." Again, our way of feeling all these things may relate to our true nature, or merely to the worldly ego.

We can feel more or less "in touch" with others and the world around us, sheltered and absorbed without losing our identity, or we can feel that we are not properly in touch. Again, these experiences, positive and negative, can be essentially secular or transcendent in character. There are major differences between feeling that only the world has abandoned us and feeling that God has abandoned us, and between feeling in touch with others and the world, and feeling—even when the world has abandoned us—that we are in touch with something beyond it.

Another significant difference is whether "being on-form" refers only to a certain external persona we put on because the world expects it of us, or whether it also—or solely—refers to the transparent outer form that matches inner form and is permeable to the Absolute. This second kind of "form," in which we are transparent, open to the Absolute, and capable of mediating it even in the hour of death is very different from the form reflected in worldly endurance, performance, and adjustment, and also from aesthetic "form."

And both can exist only unconsciously or in the consciousness of their difference.

Any state of feeling reveals its transcendent significance most clearly when it is paradoxically paired with a worldly state that contradicts it: when we are poor, and yet feel rich; are weak, and yet feel strong; fail to meet the world's demands and yet are basically on-form; have been abandoned by the world, and yet feel totally in touch. The reverse is also true: we may be rich in a worldly sense, and feel fundamentally poor; seem impressive and well-adjusted to others, and ourselves feel at odds with our true nature; belong to a sheltering worldly community, and yet be prey to deep inner loneliness. Becoming aware of these distinctions, particularly at times when absolute and worldly states are experienced as contradictory, is an important part of our work on the Way of initiation. It is precisely at times like this that we can sharpen our perception of qualities that have Being in them, gain insight into the extent to which our own general state accords with Being, or contradicts it, and finally find the right point of departure for practical exercise.

We must also learn to distinguish two kinds of transcendence: one ("Cosmos") that receives us infinitely beyond the here and now, and another ("Logos") that reaches out to touch us from a spiritual realm utterly outside the here and now. The first is maternal, warm, and dark, and encountering it is not the same thing as being summoned by the second, which is paternal, cool, and clear.

One might consider using "Life" to denote the first or female aspect, and "Being" the second or male aspect. Alternatively, "Being" and "Life" can both be used (as we have used them) to denote the transcendent One that, as *Tao*, manifests itself alternately as male and female principle *in* the yin/yang polarity. In a certain sense, however, Being (Logos) always remains above Life (Cosmos), heaven above earth—and this allows us to make a further distinction between upward and downward transcendence. Of course, the yin/yang antithesis is constantly driving toward resolution of itself in experience of the transcendent One, which lives itself out in this polarity. Indeed, it is only when we sense the Absolute in the pole toward which we are moving and the impetus that carries us toward it, that its presence remains effective in the pole we have just left.

Any experience that transcends the natural senses makes the ego-world dualism recede. There is a difference, however, depending on whether the turning point takes the form of a powerful, cosmic experience, culminating in an intoxicating, liberating unity that swallows all consciousness, or a lucid sense of being present at the point where the absolute order unfolds and a still higher consciousness is born. In this consciousness, primal life images and principles may be revealed to us—images and principles that cannot be conceptually grasped, and yet are mysteriously, brightly, illuminatingly clear to us in their all-determining significance. When this happens, we ourselves are the order we experience, and the experience itself is radiant and powerful precisely because it is not something we have, but something we *are*. Coming down to earth afterward brings subject-object dualism painfully back, and leaves us with a sad sense of having relapsed from absolute truth into a way of seeing that is natural to us, but hides the truth from us.

The experience that characterizes the objective ego is preceded by magical and mythical experience. In fact, we can distinguish four levels of human experience: 1. experience at the prepersonal level; 2. experience at the world-ego level; 3. experience in the depths of a cosmic life that is superhuman, and yet profoundly linked with human beings; and 4. experience on the highest level of true nature, which lies above all cosmic elements and reflects the Absolute. Over and above all these, as a possible fifth and quintessential level, comes an experience that follows on integration of all the other levels, that seizes us in our full extent and depth, in our individuality, and in our interconnection with the Absolute, and in which Being is fully, radiantly revealed to us against the background of our limited, everyday existence.

THE NUMINOUS AND FORM

The exercise that opens us to Being as fullness is not the same thing as the exercise that prepares us to experience Being as *inner form, order,* and *law.*

Just as Being reveals its undivided fullness chiefly through the senses (in our way of registering and perceiving ourselves and the world), so it reveals its order to us in every "meaningful form." And just as sense-perceptions can be natural or supernatural, so the experience of form can be merely secular, or can be transparent and mediate the Absolute. Bringing this distinction to consciousness is the first aim of the exercises that focus on the "formal" aspect of existence.

Supernatural Being already gleams through our lives whenever we relate to a cause, project, community, or person in a way that leaves the ego, with its self-concern and indifference to values, behind. Whenever we experience values and respond to them, a transcendent factor is at work. Logical, ethical, and aesthetic values—truth, goodness, and beauty—are the modes in which the Absolute is experienced by the world-ego and makes itself heard in the world-ego's *conscience*. Indeed, it first enters our existence when we experience values. But that experience is so totally a part of our everyday living that we fail to realize that another dimension is speaking to us when we have it. This is the point, however, at which we must start learning to perceive Being in the everyday, so that we can then move on to a proper appreciation of those special moments when it touches us outside the everyday—sometimes indeed making demands and promises that contradict the values of "natural" conscience.

Service is the basic attitudinal response to every experience of form. In every such experience, we are conscious of a whole, embodying and realizing a certain idea to a greater or lesser extent and now, as it were, *calling on* us to respect its inner meaning, protect its integrity, and help it to fulfill itself. In contact with form there is always something that forces us away from self-absorption toward dispassionate, dedicated service. In this mysterious relationship between being summoned and having to obey there is a transcendent factor, and we must learn to register it. It is conscience that enables us to do so.

Just as Being's fullness flames out briefly in every joyous sense-contact with the world, so every experience in which we respond to form—or create it—has a transcendent quality and reflects the Absolute. This is what we experience whenever the "miracle of form" addresses our *conscience*, touching us on the deepest level and inexorably compelling us to serve it. Every form, every consummated shape, can touch us like this if we let it get through to us properly, and attend to it in the right way. This is particularly true of living creatures and works of art. Above all, however, we can register Being's demands in the form that we ourselves are. For this to be possible, self-conscience as form-conscience must evolve into absolute conscience.

There are three types of conscience: The first is conscience as *fear of punishment*. This is by no means limited to children, but comes into play whenever we let possible consequences, in this life or another, regulate our conduct. Heaven and hell play a bigger part in human behavior than we might suppose. Second, conscience as the *expression of a link* with an idea, cause, or community (What the whole is determines how the parts behave). This project or community conscience speaks out whenever our actions are not (sufficiently) in tune with something to which we belong or are otherwise committed. Its central element is *honor*, which is lost by betraying our cause or community. In terms of human progress, this type of conscience already brings us closer to living from the Absolute. Third, there is *Absolute conscience*, which shows that the Absolute in our true nature is basically our only norm and yardstick. Its nature becomes clear when it forces us to do something that contradicts project or community conscience. The conflict here is between duty to the community and duty to ourselves. As ethical beings, we already know that any conflict between altruism and egoism must be decided in favor of "others" and against the ego, and the conflict between commitment to a community and commitment to true nature is equally clear-cut. We tend, however, to play it safe and opt for community commitment first—only to find, perhaps, that this choice is destroying us, or to start hearing another master's voice. This—hearing the summons that must be obeyed—is precisely the kind of experience that can first make us sense the absolute reality.

Our ability to experience the Absolute through contingent form increases as revealing Being in existence becomes the main theme in our dealings with the world—becomes, in other words, a part of our governing conscience. When conscience develops in this way, what we might term "absolute vision" can suddenly make every form stand out in a new light, lift it out of time, and simultaneously reveal in time the timeless element within it.

This absolute vision can show us two things in any given form: the timeless *idea* behind it, and its inherent *mutability*. It can see through every form to its true nature, and sometimes to the path that true nature has followed in coming to here-and-now form. The more our lives are focused on the Absolute, the more our way of experiencing form will become, in an intensified sense, our way of experiencing life in general. Indeed, the whole of life can become transparent to the idea that underlies its phenomena and the principles of growth that direct them.

Every living creature follows a secret law of growth in coming into being, moving to fulfillment, and passing out of being. In the natural vision of things, everything ends, in effect, when the third stage is reached. The more receptive we become to the Absolute, however, the more clearly we see that passing out of being is also the mysterious prelude to new form. Life's law of change is at work in this sequence, and the world-ego opposes it by aiming at finality, fixity, and permanence. From true nature's standpoint, this is the central threat to fulfillment of our destiny, which is precisely to bear witness, in contemplation and creation, to the absolute process of change. This—the great law of dying and becoming—is the eternally creative and redemptive principle in Life, and form-centered exercise must incorporate it. Form reveals its true nature only to those who are capable of dissolving form in the void, and there calling new form into being. This also holds the secret of breathing's significance in the practice of stillness.

The more we stand in otherworldly Life and live from

true nature, the less subject we are to the fixed systems in which our ordinary lives are set and play themselves out. Although we exist in space-time contingency, we are basically free of it; for we can perceive and live out the Absolute in it. There is a "simple" exercise that helps us to do this: at any point, we can give consciousness a certain twist, lift sense-data out of context, isolate, and "contemplate" them—peeling them away from the here and now and making them witness to another dimension, whose reflected glow makes us feel strangely, inviolably free.

Knowing that life continues at the very instant of dying takes us beyond the limits of what the world-ego can accept. But as this knowledge colors our whole way of seeing, life acquires a new significance, and even fixed systems cease to matter; for, once we accept change as the fundamental law, it is precisely in worldly change that the otherworldly reveals itself to us. Many people know about Life's law of dying and becoming in theory, but have never absorbed it existentially. It cannot reveal its true promise, and become the vital nerve of every exercise, until they take that further step. The meaning and purpose of ordinary living is to break the world-ego's hold. This is why dying and becoming—the process in which the old ego is dissolved in the transforming matrix, its outer forms are remade in true nature's image, and the new ego emerges from this change—is also the central element in any meditation deserving of the name.

MEDITATION

The Way of initiation is unthinkable without meditation. In the proper practice of meditation, and in the basic attitude of the person practicing, the otherworldly dimension—what Paul Tillich has called the "deep dimension"—enters consciousness, not just momentarily, but unfolding in it and remaking it at the same time.

Meditation is not something we do, but something we allow to happen. The Latin verb ("meditari") from which the word comes is a passive one, and this signifies that something is done to us—in fact, that something moves through us to the absolute center. When we meditate, we leave willed performance entirely behind, and become receptive only. Meditation is not a matter of focusing on something, but of being focused by something. It is not a matter of confronting something, but of uniting with it. It is true that we always start the exercise by "concentrating," actively "withdrawing from our surroundings," and "collecting ourselves" inwardly. But real meditation—meditation as state—begins only when this preliminary phase has been completed.

Meditation is not objective contemplation of some "outside thing"—an image, word, or thought. As we have said, it is never a matter of confronting a definite *something*, but of fusing with it. This is why the "how" of meditation is more important than the "what"—provided that we use it as an "exercise on the Way," and not for some practical purpose, such as improving our concentration.

If meditation, like every exercise on the Way, ultimately sets out to make us permeable to Being, and if this basic purpose infuses our whole attitude, then the content of objective consciousness is less important than the fact of overcoming it. In meditation, objective confrontation always yields to subjective integration, as we peel ourselves away from the multiplicity of surface consciousness and move toward the undivided fullness of the depths. Regardless of the "object" we start from, meditation allows us to break through here-and-now systems, and experience ourselves in a wholly new dimension, in which there is depth without content. If we really have the courage to do this, it also enables us to throw off empty forms and renew our beliefs by aligning them on the otherworldly fullness that constitutes their real meaning. "Meditari," being traveled to the center, ultimately brings us to our soul's innermost core. In fact, when we meditate, we are being led home to the primal source and wellspring. This is an element that does not simply offer us a refuge from the tensions of the surface. It also releases us to new form and, having made us over and recharged us, sends us back into the world. This "inner haven" is always waiting to receive us, and it can mean two things: a place of final homecoming, and a place of fresh departure. What it becomes for us depends on what we look for in it: final dissolution and return, or transformation and a new beginning. Reconnecting with the otherworldly source can be either happy ending or hopeful start.

Only those who know nothing about meditation, or have never experienced it properly, can make the common mistake of saying that seated meditation and the other meditation practices merely lure those who follow them into typically Oriental escapism. First of all, the East is not interested in escaping from the world, but in overcoming it*; this is the necessary prelude to mastering it properly. Secondly, fusion

* Cf. Lama Anagarika Govinda: *Grundlagen tibetischer Mystik* (Weilheim/Obb.: O. W. Barth, 3rd edition, 1972).

with the All-One does not necessarily mean once-and-for-all dissolution. It can also provide a point of departure for renewed acceptance, confrontation, and shaping of the world —can, in other words, give birth to a person who maintains contact with Being *in* his or her way of relating to the world.

Anyone practicing meditation with total dedication finds, at a certain point, that the process suddenly tips over into a special kind of *activity*—an activity that comes from the innermost depths, expresses the primal "élan vital," and has nothing whatever to do with egocentric, volitional, and objective forms of action. This shift marks the transition in meditation from a passive and redeeming mode to an active and creating one. Meditation also leads to relinquishment of all the well-worn paths and rigid structures that stand in the way of maturity, renewal, and primal action. *Surrender of the created wakes the uncreated in ourselves.* It is precisely the uncreated that is the source of all genuinely creative existence, endeavor, and action. This insight underlies those ancient Japanese skills that are practiced on the Way, and in which perfected technique allows adepts to leave the ego behind and hand themselves over to true nature—that uncreated matrix from which the Absolute now erupts. No longer held in check by the self-seeking, angst-ridden ego, it reveals itself joyously in consummate achievement and performance, which are no longer "done," but flower unaided from the depths, and are thus genuinely creative.

This link between release from the created and renewal from the uncreated is also something that anyone practicing Zen-style seated meditation—*zazen*—can experience.* Here, too, the adept has no definite "object" of meditation. He or

---

* Cf. Hakuin Yasutani: "Za-Zen" in Dürckheim, *Wunderbare Katze* (Weilheim/Obb.: O. W. Barth, 1964).

she relies on such an object, e.g., breathing or rhythmic counting, only in the concentration phase that precedes meditation. Later, all of this is discarded as the threshold of something that "transcends" the old ego is approached.

The only way of experiencing Being through form is to experience form itself as *unique* and separate. Just as All-One-Being reveals itself vitally to us only in our individuality, and never comes home as genuine inner experience if we try to ignore that individuality, so we can experience the numinous character of the forms we encounter only if they touch us directly in their uniqueness. This is why dream archetypes are numinous only in "symbolic" images that concentrate the dreamer's life and experience in their here-and-now uniqueness. Conversely, images become numinous only when a higher order, another dimension, manifests itself and shines out in them.

The miracle of Being reveals itself only in the unique, and every stereotype and generalization robs it of the power to do so. Conversely, even the habitual and long-familiar can show us the Absolute when it suddenly touches us with the magic of the primal and unique. Thus the bell I have heard a hundred times, the tree I see outside my window every day, the well-known gestures of my life-companion—anything and anyone can become the voice of Being, when that thing or person touches me "primally," that is, touches me directly at this very time, in this very place, and in this very way. And whenever Being touches us, the totally familiar becomes a primal happening. This is why it is important to develop an overall attitude and consciousness in which the forms we are given to realize are repeatedly stripped of the veils of habit and conceptual significance, and are enabled to touch us directly.

The Absolute touches us only in the unique, but the

unique witnesses to the Absolute only to the extent that it is also experienced and "enters" us as a manifestation of the All-One. In the ascending hierarchy of normal concepts, the "All-One" is the most abstract of all. On the descending scale of experiences that plumb our personal depths, however, it is the most concrete. It is our most personal, innermost life in its supreme form—is quite simply the power that transforms us. It is "we ourselves" in our true nature. And so we experience it from the ego as the deepest thing in us, and also as the element in which we are rooted and sheltered in a total sense. Whenever Being is truly experienced, however, ego and true nature merge and coincide.

The exercise in which we practice sensing the All-One in and through the particular is a special one. As this attitude infuses our daily living, a contrapuntal relationship is established, with the Absolute's music ringing out in the contingent. The *radiance* of form also depends on the uniqueness that denotes the All-One's presence. It vanishes whenever convention or purposive conformity eliminates uniqueness. We, too, are radiant in this sense only when we avoid conformity, compromise, stereotyping, and routine, and succeed in being repeatedly, newly present in the here and now from our individuality's creative center. "Right" form always gives us the freedom to do this, whereas "good" form, which is merely copied and assumed, robs us of that freedom.

Once we have started to understand how All-One-Being relates to the universal principles and figures of Life in which it touches us, and also to every Life-form's individuality, we can make this insight the basis of a special kind of exercise— those exercises, for instance, in which certain primal gestures are repeated alertly and consciously.

Consciously encountering the primal figures of existence focuses the experience of true nature's individuality and brings it to living consciousness. This insight underlies the *exercise of guided drawing** developed by Maria Hippius, in which students learn to draw certain basic forms—circles, waves, spirals, rectangles, curves, asterisks, closed and open figures—over and over again with total concentration, eventually becoming part of the activity in a way that wakes the universal principle of form in themselves. If they really succeed in fusing with the activity, so that it is no longer performed objectively, but subjectively, they may find that it brings their true nature's individuality to consciousness through all the screens of here-and-now contingency. For the basic existential pattern, which helps to determine their own being, is present in them only in their own unique and personal mode. When they "complete" it in a lengthy, meditative process of repetition, their true nature's individuality enters consciousness in and through it, redeeming them from the old ego and liberating them to new form.

Being can also, as it were, flare up in existence and touch our own true nature when we respond to form and accept it. A flower's form, for example, can allow its true nature, or numen, to show through, giving our experience of it a numinous quality that strikes a chord in our own true nature. This kind of experience, too, can be the purpose of meditative stillness and contemplation.

The "fullness of Being" is always experienced as a sustaining, vitalizing, and renewing *energy* that seems to defy all the limitations and perils of here-and-now existence. Being as "order and form" is always experienced as a *light*** that dispels the darkness of contingency, revealing the essential and eliminating the irrelevant.

This is the light that brings forms and formal order out

* Cf. Maria Hippius: "Beitrag aus der Werkstatt," in M. Hippius (ed.), *Transzendenz als Erfahrung*, O. W. Barth, Weilheim/Obb. 1966.
** Cf. Jean Gebser: "Vermutungen über das unerschaffene Licht," in *Transzendenz als Erfahrung* (Weilheim/Obb.: O. W. Barth, 1966).

of the darkness for the first time. When Being is experienced as otherworldly order, life is illuminated, existence clarified, and a meaning revealed that lies beyond meaning and unmeaning in the normal sense. This clarity is not clarity about something, but a state of being clear—a "standing in the light." It witnesses to Being with special force at those turning points where it suddenly illuminates existential darkness, and the Absolute shines out as ultimate meaning, unexpectedly saving us from despair at the world's absurdity.

Whenever we are transparent ourselves, existence becomes transparent too—and another *order* gleams mysteriously through its apparent chaos. When this happens, we suddenly "see" ourselves in a new light, and are lifted out of the darkness. Being in this state brings us our clearest perception of transparency's dependence on a very special balance between inner and outer form. At one time, we feel "together," at another less so, and we can learn and practice ways of looking critically into ourselves and seeing how the inner process of coming to form is progressing. When outer (body) and inner (spirit) are in tune, we attain a state of total bliss, in which bodily order expresses and realizes spiritual order, while spiritual order incorporates and realizes bodily order.* As the French might put it, "l'ordre du coeur" is reflected and fulfilled in "l'ordre du corps."

In every true contact with Being through form, there is not only something that redeems us, but also something that imposes certain obligations on us. Experiencing Being through form, order, and law fills us with the gladdening promise of an order that transcends the here and now, and also wakes the conscience that makes us work toward right form in the here and now. Every experience of form that allows Being to

---

* Cf. M. Hippius: *Transzendenz als Erfahrung*, loc. cit., p. 30.

show through wakes us from the sleep of habit, and, as it were, propels us into a new process of doing and becoming.

THE NUMINOUS AND LOVE

The exercise that prepares us to experience Being in its third aspect focuses on Being as otherworldly, all-uniting, all-embracing, and all-sheltering *unity*.

The possibility of being touched by "Being as unity" exists whenever *union* is sought, accepted, lived, and joyously experienced—but also whenever all of this is agonizingly absent. Indeed, it is precisely when life shows us its cruelest face—when we feel forsaken, friendless, and alone—that Being can paradoxically flower from the depths of unbearable anguish, sheltering and warming us against the world's coldness.

Union always has a special otherworldly character, and we often experience that quality most forcefully when we are utterly alone—and can taste Being's nature and presence *in* its absence. Of course, we then experience it again in a very special sense when worldly solitude swings over into otherworldly security. And so it is at the very point where everyday separations and divisions become unbearable that we can experience the unity of Being—only to experience it in an even deeper sense when those separations and divisions are overcome. The important thing is not to pass these moments by, but to be alert to their special, otherworldly quality, and capable of surrendering to it, so that it can open us increasingly to the Absolute.

The experience of Being as primal unity is not limited to exceptional situations, but can come whenever we emerge from the self-shielding ego's isolation—whenever self-assertion turns into self-surrender. Indeed, even loners, who sometimes lose their lease on life completely, stand a special chance of suddenly experiencing Being as unity if they can only step outside the ego and really reach out to something else.

True union with a thing or person always has an inner quality, a potentially numinous center, in which absolute unity rings out and reveals itself. This quality gives the experience itself a significance that lifts it above the merely here-and-now, while a warm wave from the depths carries the person having the experience—perhaps only for a split second, but unmistakably—into another, broader reality.

Love is Being's chief medium for numinous revelation of itself as unity in human consciousness. Every relationship that can properly be termed a love relationship offers the opportunity of sensing Being in existence.

Whenever we use the word *love* correctly—of things, animals, people, God, or even ourselves in our true nature—we are conscious both of a fundamental unifying connection with the love-object, and also, because we are nonetheless separate, of an urge to unite with it. It is uniting with someone or something in this way that offers us the chance of savoring fundamental unity in a numinous sense—and the chance increases as we learn to see every such union as a manifestation of the Unity in which all true natures are rooted and connected.

It is not simply at the moment of union that we can sense the underlying unity of Being—even separation can have the same effect. When people who love each other are parted, their very separation, and longing for each other are charged with an absolute quality, a painful and yet gladdening energy. The same is true of the exile's longing for home.

Just as anguish at being separated from otherworldly Life is undoubtedly the most basic form of human suffering, so the urge to be reunited with it is the most basic human longing. And this is precisely why love, which is always composed of union and separation, is also the field in which the otherworldly can touch us most easily—always assuming that we are predisposed to experience its presence.

It is not simply union, fusion, and liberation from the agony of separation that can have a sacred quality. That quality can also inhere in the coming-to-oneself, the realization of creative potential, which union always involves. Above all, however, it is present in the experience of genuine communion, which becomes possible for the first time when two people fulfill themselves by uniting, and go on to experience a higher unity in each other. Similarly, it is not simply the experience of unity after separation that is filled with Being, but equally the moment when unity experienced in the radiance of another's love brings one's own true nature miraculously to consciousness. This supreme form of love throws a clarifying light on all human relationships and on the possibility, present in them as their deepest meaning, of Being's becoming an inner presence. For Being to speak out in human relationships, however, those relationships must be free of any pragmatic coloring.

In existence, love is the great educator toward Being; for it constantly counters the self-shielding ego, which is permanently focused on its own worldly position, and cannot yield, let go, accept, or surrender. With its tendency toward stasis and self-isolation, that ego is the great adversary of Being, the universal reconciler, and the possibility of experiencing Being in ourselves.

Life is filled with moments of union, and thus with opportunities of experiencing the Absolute consciously in them. We must simply learn to see experienced unity and union for what they are, and to internalize their special quality against the background of earlier division. One way of doing this is to practice becoming one with an instrument or implement we use for a specific art, craft, or purpose (e.g., the typewriter I am using at this moment). When we give ourselves completely to a task imposed on us (and possibly resented to start with), suddenly solve a brain-racking problem, or stop resisting something and accept it—in all of this we can sense and savor unity. It is precisely because our ordinary lives rest entirely on the ego that excludes us from the absolute unity for which we long, consciously or unconsciously, in our true nature, that even the briefest experience of union can become an experience of Being, an experience that is also available in any familiar activity.

There is a quiet and careful way of performing habitual actions, using long-familiar instruments, and pacing out daily followed tracks that can make us feel part of a harmonious process, and touch us on the deepest level as a greeting from absolute unity.

There is a way of exercising a practiced skill in which knowing that we have to do this very thing, at this very moment, in this very manner conjures up something in which consciousness of absolute unity is at work. Admittedly, ego-world consciousness points firmly in the opposite direction, and normally costs us the opportunity but, if manifestation of Being in existence is our deepest concern, the longing to experience absolute unity steadily intensifies, and every moment and sense of worldly union becomes part of the great exercise. And so we can learn to let ourselves merge with the things we see, hear, say, taste, and sense in such a way that the antithesis between seer and seen, hearer and heard, etc., disappears, and pure seeing and hearing fill our consciousness, making it witness to fundamental unity in the language of that particular moment.

One useful exercise here is to practice seeing the inner meaning of diffuse, uncontoured form. Dusk, moonlight, misty landscapes, and even the dancing brilliance of noon, when outlines blur in the shimmering light, all lend themselves to this. As the contrasts fade into silence, the stillness of primal unity can be heard in all of them. Also relevant are exercises in which we immerse ourselves in undifferentiated sound—the booming of a waterfall, the indefinable rustling of a forest, or even the high-impact cacophony of urban living. First, however, we must master the art of pausing and retreating into a state of inner looking and listening in which we no longer look *at* or listen *to* anything, and for that very reason can hear the otherworldly counterpoint in which all the noises of everyday living blend in a music that tells us of the Absolute.

Practicing on forms whose meaning depends on *counterform* is particularly effective. An example of this is those Oriental ink drawings in which the pictured form serves only to evoke nonform, and so make form itself transparent to the primal ground, from which everything comes, and to which it returns. This exercise helps us to overcome our tendency to define objectively or surrender to mere feeling, and move on to an experience in which the antitheses of form and nonform, world and nonworld are destroyed, and yet preserved in a way that allows the supra-antithetical One to show through them. At this stage, we are dealing with something that is neither form, nor nonform, but lies beyond that antithesis.

At first, trying to focus consciously on the absolute content of moments of union, those moments of loving surrender that redeem us from division, seems bizarre and unnatural. Surely this is destroying the treasure they contain? This would indeed be the case if "coming to consciousness" were always synonymous with the way in which rational systems bring "objects" to consciousness. Turning us in on ourselves and marking us off from our surroundings, that kind of consciousness also lifts us out of Being, and indeed conceals it from us. Hence the common and damaging mistake made by many sects, when they confuse alertness to Being with that rational alertness that defines the given, incorporates it into an existing system, and reduces it to something that can be manipulated. When we are experiencing Being, we may well "recognize" what is happening and realize its significance, but recognition in this case is waking union, and not distancing definition. This is where the meaning of "coming to consciousness" becomes important. There are actually two ways of perceiving: one orders experience conceptually, while the other incorporates it into the perceiver's own "Way-body," which grows as Being increasingly becomes an inner presence.

"Trying to comprehend the incomprehensible does not destroy its absolute quality if the consciousness that clarifies and illuminates the situation springs from the same absolute dimension as the initial, intensified experience. This consciousness is *light*, forcing its way into the shadow-world within and providing a focus for the raising and saving of the treasures of a sense-experience that transcends the senses. The element which had previously been the dark, maternal ground's ungrown child is illuminated and rendered transparent. Awareness of higher order brings the birth of the 'spiritual spirit,' enlightened consciousness, and with it the primal light strikes a spark in the individual."*

Both we and our coming to form on the Way follow a personal law of becoming, and this law allows us to see every

* Cf. M. Hippius: *Transzendenz als Erfahrung*, loc. cit., p. 33.

moment in life as a specific stage in the process—as it were, to perceive its "value" in those terms. The consciousness that operates here does not focus on "objects," but expresses the Way's inner presence in the body. It does not destroy the absolute substance of experience, but preserves it—and indeed deepens it as well, both illuminating and completing the inner order. This process of "coming to consciousness" makes us more receptive to the Absolute, and at the same time more mature, and more capable of being penetrated and transformed by it. It allows us to open ourselves to the depths while remaining on the level of objective consciousness. In meditation—*zazen*, for instance—we can thus be unwaveringly focused on maintaining right posture and yet be "somewhere else" in deeper consciousness, and aware of the signs that our general attitude is right: a strange inner strength, a warming of the body, a slight tension in the spinal column, a brightening of the spirit, a filling with love—often coming in "waves" that are utterly gentle, yet wholly unmistakable, and all pointing to gradual accomplishment of a total change in which absolute fullness, radiance, and warmth infuse us and lift us out of our normal existential state. Developing our capacity for this kind of inner perception is a part of that inner growing toward right "form," in which we become increasingly permeable to the Absolute, that is, increasingly capable of experiencing otherworldly fullness, order, and unity, and witnessing to them in the world. Practicing to contact Being in the numinous aspects of sense, form, and love is a permanent part of the Way of initiation.

The primal sense of Life both precedes and transcends everything we perceive and register as making formal sense through our physical senses. "Sense" here means both the meaning we can discern and must fulfill, and the physical organs through which it comes home to us. Ultimately, the exercises that teach us to see absolute fullness, order, and

unity in the numinous also make us capable of sensing otherworldly strength, meaning, and love in the midst of worldly
peril, absurdity, and lovelessness.

The sense that life can have, and the sense with which
we register it, coincide at start and finish. Our very way of
"being there" expresses the Absolute's presence whenever we
are in touch with it—and to the extent that we are in touch
with it. On the Way, the thing we seek is always the motive
force behind our seeking, and so Being itself is already at work
whenever we turn toward it. And whenever we turn toward
it in a total sense, we ourselves coincide with it. The effective,
illuminating, and all-uniting primal meaning of life is life itself.

WHAT IT ALL
LEADS TO

COMPASSION:
HUMANS–FELLOW HUMANS

In the era that is now drawing to a close, "compassion" has never been a popular word. It has always been at odds with the ethic of a world ruled by reason, and still is today. That ethic is hard, soulless, and objective. It has no time for the heart, and finds "compassion" too warm, too soft, too close to pity. It brackets it with "charity," another word that makes people uncomfortable, either because it reminds them of neglected duties and gives them a bad conscience, or because they are interested only in their rights, and reject anything that smacks of pity.

When we rediscover ourselves, we also rediscover others—in terms of both partnership and responsibility. We are built for dialogue. Human life is essentially a matter of summons and reply: world to world, person to person. Very few people seem to realize, however, that the divine summons: "Adam, where art thou?" lies outside the normal pattern, and that we become fully human only by responding to *that* summons—the summons of the Absolute. We also need to learn again that personal relationships are right in the deepest sense only when Being is their ultimate determinant. For human life fulfills itself completely only when our human relationships serve their real purpose: revealing the other-worldly in the world in other people. There are many things, however, that prevent this from happening.

At first, no general definition of the purpose of relating to others in the right way seems possible, since relationships are infinitely varied, and each has its own concerns and problems. Quite apart from the fact that no two individual relationships are alike, the various category relationships—parent/child, husband/wife, doctor/patient, employer/employee, teacher/pupil, priest/parishioner—seem to have nothing in common. In every one, the focus is different. And yet there is something that connects them all.

People can meet in various circumstances, roles, and situations, but the basic encounter is always between two *human beings*, and each has a human responsibility to the other. Behind all the roles, there are human beings, with the same urge, obligation, and longing to realize themselves as human beings—and indeed as very specific human beings. In every human being, we encounter life—and also Life, which is present in everyone's true nature. This is why every human relationship carries the possibility of making it easier or harder for others to manifest the Absolute, of helping them to fulfill their human destiny or failing to do so.

Ultimately, compassion involves helping others to reach and remain in a state that allows them to manifest, preserve, and transmit otherworldly Life in their own lives and in their own way. The full implications of this as possibility and obligation become clear only when Being is seen and comes home to us in its threefold unity: as primal plenitude, prescribed order, and all-connecting unity. All life (including all human life) depends on this triunity, and the basic purpose of every revolution (including today's revolution of the young) is to restore the conditions in which it can manifest itself—supporting, clarifying, protecting—in our existence.

Otherworldly Life manifests itself in human beings as primal, overflowing energy, as primal impulse toward form and order, and as primal longing for wholeness and security—for love. True nature's urge to fulfill itself in these three respects determines the whole of human life, and all human suffering can be traced to its failure to do so in one of them—a fact we must never forget. And so these primal aims are also the focus of all true compassion.

The elemental urge to experience absolute fullness is contradicted by the perils of a world that threatens to destroy us and fills us with terror. To show compassion here is to take other people's fears seriously and help to remove them. The longing to give existence a meaning by harmonizing outer form with inner form is contradicted by the injustice and lawlessness of a world that makes us despair. To show compassion here is to recognize this despair and try to relieve it. The longing for fellowship, security, and love is contradicted by the cruelty of a world that condemns us to loneliness. To show compassion here is to feel others' solitude and help them to escape from it. Whatever the roles in which people meet, one of these three types of anguish is always present—and so is the possibility of showing compassion.

Seeing or treating people as things, objects, bits of the world, makes compassion impossible. This is what happens, for example, when medical patients are treated as "cases," when workers are treated as "productive units," and when children in school are treated as "pupils"—and not as human beings, subjects, or persons.

As persons, we are part of a system whose meaning and values cannot be grasped by reason alone or deduced from the world's objective demands, for our normal way of seeing makes the experiencing, suffering, and hoping subject the focal point of life. In personal terms, the issue is promise and fulfillment, suffering and redemption from suffering, failure or success in realizing the self—in short, growing and maturing on the inner way. To show compassion here is to walk beside another person on his or her inner way.

At every stage in our development, compassion means something different—just as the triunity of the living Absolute, and the primal purposes and sufferings that are rooted in it, mean different things for the child, the adult, and finally the man or woman who has matured into personhood. At every stage, we hope for—and need—different things from other people.

Children are at the premental stage, and still a part of Life's primal wholeness. They are still firmly anchored in Being, and the bond is typically expressed, while it remains intact, in a basic confidence in life, an unquestioning faith in a necessary, meaningful order, and a sense of being totally shielded and safe. Only to the extent that they meet these primal expectations do parents discharge their human responsibility to their children. When—to take only the most common mistakes—they undermine their children's instinctive faith in the sustaining powers of life by being over-strict, ride roughshod over their children's individual true natures with their preconceived childrearing notions, or starve the primal need for security by not loving them enough and throwing them back on themselves, the primal contact with Being is broken. The child then reacts by adjusting in ways that shield him or her from the hazards, injustice, and coldness of a world that contradicts true nature. While it is true that these adjustments help to minimize the pain of living, they also stifle true nature's primal impulses. Once they set hard, they form the deepest root-bed of the neuroses that surface in the angst, guilt, and relational problems of adulthood. Most of these are traceable to the stifling of true nature in early childhood, when parents, usually without knowing it, failed to show the right kind of compassion. Conversely, whenever a person has a confidence in life, a belief in order, and a sense of security that no danger, injustice, or solitude can shake, we can be sure that his or her primal needs were satisfied in childhood . . . or that personal maturity has allowed him or her to rediscover the absolute roots that were buried at that stage.

Parental failure or damaging experience in later life are not the only causes of separation from the Absolute. Our natural human development contains a factor that threatens the primal link: the rise of rational consciousness. Part of our normal growth process is emergence of the ego that makes us self-reliant, and also makes us see ourselves as the masters or servants of an independent outside world. This ego is an inescapable feature of the human condition, and, however strong or weak our primal link with the Absolute may be, we cannot be fully self-conscious without relying on it—without believing that we have, know, and can do enough to satisfy most of the world's demands. This is why compassion in relation to children also involves helping them to build viable world-egos, to express and fulfill themselves in effort, achievement, and human relations, and to develop the qualities they need for all of this. Growth of the ego in this sense is particularly dependent on a special kind of compassion. Discouragement inhibits it quite as much as mollycoddling. And so compassion here involves trusting, encouraging, and loving the child, waking his or her abilities, and allowing those abilities to open and test themselves on the obstacles that mark each stage in the process. Child raising is the art of productive resistance.

The decisive factor in development of the right ego is sustaining affirmation of Life.

The root-force of all human existence is the divine "élan vital" that sustains every living creature and leads it to fulfillment of its destiny. In human beings, it takes the form of an instinctive, unconscious "yes" to life in general—but it does not become really beneficial and creative until we consciously say "yes" to our own particular lives.

This instinctive life-affirmation is jeopardized when children's primal needs are suppressed, when they themselves are unwanted, or when traumatic experiences make them feel rejected, excluded, violated, or forsaken, and discouragement, lack of understanding, or lovelessness throw them back upon themselves. Conversely, the life climate is beneficial when people are made to feel from childhood on that they are valued, understood, and accepted for what they are. Our saying "yes" to life, and thus our whole self-consciousness, is partly dependent on the world's saying "yes" or "no" to us. Consciousness of self is something that other people always help to build.

Self-consciousness follows the triunity of Being in having three root-forms: consciousness of our own strength, consciousness of our own value, and consciousness of ourselves as members of a community.

If the primal link with Being comes through childhood unbroken, we are left with an unshakable consciousness of our own strength, an invincible trust in ourselves and in life. Similarly, if our individuality has developed unhindered, we are left with a consciousness of our own value that does not depend on how others see us, and is not damaged when the verdict goes against us. And we also have an enduring sense of being primally connected, fundamentally in touch, with everything and everyone, and so protected against loneliness or solitude. This primal self-consciousness is rooted in true nature and beyond the world's grasp, and we cannot preserve it unless the key figures in childhood—our parents—show the right compassion and keep our roots in Being intact.

As children become adults and the independent world-ego develops, contact with otherworldly true nature relaxes. They are forced to rely on themselves in thinking the world out and coping with it in practice, and they feel increasingly dependent on it—all the more so if the primal connection with the Absolute has already been lost in childhood. Compassion at this stage means helping them to realize the three basic impulses of Life in the world-ego's language—helping them to live securely, serve a cause or community meaningfully, and find satisfaction in true human contact with their fellows. These are abstract requirements, and each must be satisfied in its own way, but every role and situation in which we meet others gives us an opportunity to bring compassion to bear on their worldly existence, and them the opportunity of doing the same for us. We need only remember that the obligation exists. But to satisfy the duty of compassion in this way is by no means to exhaust the possibilities and obligations inherent in it.

Just as people are not their world-egos, but become fully themselves only by connecting consciously with their otherworldly true nature, so compassion is compassion in the deepest sense only when it takes true nature as its reference point. And so there is a vital distinction between the compassion we owe the suffering world-ego, and the compassion we owe true nature, when the world-ego overshadows or suppresses it. To show compassion in this second sense is to accompany another person on his or her way to maturity.

Every human relationship—in the family, in everyday life, or at work—offers us the opportunity of accompanying and helping others, and relieving not only their worldly anguish, but their true nature's anguish as well. There is always a danger, however, of seeing others in their worldly roles only, and overlooking their true nature's needs. This happens, for example, when parents see only "sons" or "daughters" in their children, and dismiss all the things that make them unique as "cute" or "crazy"—frequently allowing ready-made child-rearing theories to stifle the development process demanded by true nature. The damage extends into adult life if later authority figures rate the individual solely in terms of the job or function he or she performs. All of this blocks the truly decisive developmental factor, and ensures that the secret longing for space in which true nature can unfold—the longing that reflects our deepest human aspiration—remains unsatisfied. And so treating other people as brothers and sisters in the Absolute is the key to true compassion, the compassion that breaks through the agonizing confines of world-ego reality's never-ending circle. This is where our era's real opportunity—and, in a certain sense, new obligation—begins.

Fully rounded personality has so far been the ordinary human ideal, but the aim today is *personal* development. The ideal of personality is realized by people who are both successful in a worldly sense and able to serve a cause and community effectively. This ideal is also bound up with certain conceptions of honor and freedom: the honor displayed in loyally defending certain values, and the freedom won by overcoming basic human nature and the puny ego, and selflessly serving a cause. So far, it has been possible to regard this kind of service as the highest human endeavor because worldly achievement, and particularly the sustaining forms of community, have also been humanly valid in the deepest sense. They have carried and shielded the whole person—and so carried and shielded his or her transcendent center too.

This metaphysical dimension is lost, however, once a community becomes an organized structure, in which people can keep going only by losing themselves utterly in their purely human concerns. Sensual possibility and objective performance then survive as the only realities, and self-reliance becomes the keynote of everyone's humanity. But it is precisely here that our true responsibility for our fellow humans begins—all the more so since the world's denial of our needs wakes us to the otherworldly. This indeed is the special feature of our age—the Absolute is beginning to enter consciousness, and we are breaking through the limits of ordinary consciousness to the exact extent that the worldly forces we encounter in that consciousness are impeding and frustrating us. It is as if a new life were dawning, and the sun rising on a moonlit landscape, revealing it clearly for the first time. And this is where compassion's real and greatest task begins: helping others to discover otherworldly Life in themselves and then in the true nature of everything around them, and to find strength in that discovery to advance to the higher human level on which they attain true personhood. To be a person in this sense is to be transparent to Being, and capable of manifesting it in radiant experience, the charisma of unobstructed Life-form, and the positive effects of everything one does.

COMPASSION AND
DOCTORS

Every therapy reflects a specific conception of what people are
and what they are meant to be. When this conception changes,
therapy shifts its sights, and health is also redefined. Our
ideas on human beings are changing today, and this change
is reflected in the crisis through which Western medicine is
passing. On the one hand, the modern tendency to rationalize
life—and medicine—and forget about the person is being carried to extremes; on the other, this depersonalization of life
is provoking a reaction, and the individual is waking as
person—and waking in the doctor's surgery as well. Hence
the new challenge that medicine is confronting.

In the meantime, however, the rationalization of life—
and medicine—continues. The methods of scientific medicine
are developing and being refined all the time, with ever more
spectacular results. Alarmingly, the human relationship between doctor and patient is also giving way increasingly to a
purely objective relationship, in which a "medical profession"
or "medical team" (a specialized collective) provides an in-

sured and organized "patient body" with the impersonal, scientific services to which it has a defined legal right. The objective organizations that control communications, the economy, and industry today are now clearly mirrored in the workings of "organized health," and "health" itself simply means the ability to serve those organizations reliably, and to meet the impersonal requirements of a world that sees people as "objects" and is interested only in "results."

The very inhumanity of this world can, however, wake people as "subjects." When it does this, it also wakes the human being in the patient, and the person in the human being—and the person insists on being taken seriously and treated as a person, and refuses to be treated as a "case." This change revolutionizes healing as well, and initiates the transformation to personal medicine.

Rational, world-centered consciousness sees human beings as things and treats them accordingly. The "thing" that conventional medicine addresses is the physical (more recently psychophysical) organism, and its disorders are diagnosed at a scientific distance, treated impersonally, and rectified with minimum delay, so that the patient can get on with his or her worldly tasks.

It is, of course, true that people are part of the "world," and must sometimes be treated with worldly methods for worldly ends. But whole human beings are not just parts in the sense of objectively mendable components. They are personal subjects, and the things that can be rationally grasped and treated are only one aspect of their personal living. Indeed, even those things can ultimately be seen and treated properly only from the standpoint of personal wholeness.

The system of coordinates we live in as personal subjects is not the world's system, which is fixed in space and time, and determined by objective causes. This second system is external and objective, whereas the first is internal and subjective, and operates on three levels. The first is the level of the body, on which biological laws apply from cradle to grave. The second is the level of the ego, on which suffering and redemption from suffering, promise and fulfillment, and potential and actual realization of the self are the issues. On this level, we experience pain and joy, success and failure as we grow and develop in our own particular setting, at our own particular rate, in our own particular body, and confront destruction, despair, loneliness, and death in our quest for a life that is pain-free, happy, and secure. As this "I," we depend on a "you"—on the understanding, assistance, and compassion of others—and we also expect compassion from doctors. The third level is the level of true nature, on which we transcend both the body and the world-ego, and seek to develop our true nature in contact with otherworldly Life. Here again, there are tasks for the medical practitioner.

Today's doctors must realize that the sufferings of people who are struggling into personhood are not simply physical, and not simply the result of failing to serve a cause and community effectively, but are a result on a far deeper level of the anguish of frustrated true nature, as it strives to fulfill itself and achieve right form in the face of all worldly obstacles and of pain itself. Compassion and understanding are not enough for true nature. It wants to be summoned, guided, and accompanied on the inner way—and it wants all of this from doctors too.

Personhood is our intended destiny, and we fulfill it in the never-ending transition from a worldly subjective state, which is limited to the world-ego, to an otherworldly subjective state, which is rooted in true nature. To achieve the changeover is to follow the *personal law* written into every one of us, and medicine does not become personal medicine until doctors stop seeing their patients as "cases," and start seeing them in terms of that personal law—are no longer content to tackle their world-ego's problems with ordinary compassion, but do everything they can to accompany them on the way to personhood as well.

Conventional "health" is simply the ability to function painlessly and effectively in a worldly sense, and to keep on doing so—but personal medicine broadens the concept to "wholeness." Wholeness in this sense is the overall state in which we follow true nature's demands and remain on the path of progressive change toward becoming divine subjects and being "in good order"—not from and for the world, but from and for God. Seen in this light, personal medicine—like every truly personal conception of human beings—is fundamentally religious, or "initiatory." This is not to connect it with specific religions or confessions, or to suggest that it should supplement conventional diagnosis and treatment with religious methods or practices. What it means is that doctors, regardless of the problem they are treating, should focus on their patients' otherworldly center, and do everything possible to assist them with reference to their personal law.

Personal medicine is not the same thing as applied psychology. Biological/physiological and psychological treatment can both miss the patient as personal subject—for example, when psychological treatment merely tries, like any other branch of impersonal, specialized medicine, to restore worldly function. Any form of treatment that concentrates solely on eliminating pain and keeping people comfortable disregards their true nature, and thus their real purpose in life. This is what one writer meant when he spoke of "a medicine and therapy that obstruct the individual's capacity for cure by tumbling him into harmful good health."*

Every physical illness subverts or destroys the natural

---

* Cf. H. Müller-Eckhard: *Von der Krankheit, nicht krank sein zu können*, Stuttgart: Klett.

ego's plan and system. Its disruptive effect in this sense is undoubted—but so is the opportunity it offers of connecting with the Absolute. The more startling, radical, and hopeless a disease is, the more fiercely the natural ego resists it. But its frantic eagerness to eliminate pain and get back to normal prevents the hidden forces of the deep from helping us, and stops us from hearing true nature's voice. True nature is never content to remove the symptoms, but wants to turn the whole person round and lead him or her to maturity. The hardened, ambitious, self-assertive world-ego is not merely the psychic root of most human illness, but stands in the way of any real cure—and so breaking down its resistance is always a part of the doctor's task.

Once doctors understand that partnering the natural ego is not their only role, and that they have a duty to focus on their patients' true nature and "personal process of becoming" as well, then—whatever the illness—wholly new possibilities and tasks open up. It is precisely when a patient's ability to accept, understand, and endure is strained to the breaking point that true nature's power and potential may wake and, if that patient reacts correctly, bring their healing energies to bear. If the sick person only accepts what is happening in the right way, then darkness, bewilderment, and impotence can themselves become the source of illumination and healing. Doctors can contribute here by helping their patients to face up bravely to the things they cannot understand, and to wait confidently and quietly, instead of rebelling. To do this, of course, doctors must have this ability themselves, and must know from their own experience that the healing spirit is at work in the very heart of the incomprehensible. The "personal" doctor does not simply summon the natural forces of the patient's spirit and will, but opens his or her heart to receive the inflowing primal energies as well. Under their influence, impatience, tension, and fear disappear and, as the personal subject is healed, physical cure also progresses more quickly. This is why knowing about the transforming and healing power of the trust that keeps people going when disease has left them helpless is an essential part of living personal medicine. Doctors who can open up the spring of supernatural trust in their patients, and turn natural resistance to illness into an impulse toward further progress on the inner Way, unleash a healing process that goes far beyond the mere restoration of lost function.

Doctors who practice personal medicine in this sense may seem to be overstepping the "medical" limits of their profession. On the contrary, they are practicing their profession fully for the first time. Their medical and psychological knowledge, their experience and insight, and their traditional medical skills are not being left behind, but are being applied for the first time in that wider sense that matches individual wholeness. When doctors subordinate everything they do to the patient's personal law, they are not limiting the traditional methods of research and treatment, but refining and deepening them. Indeed, conventional physical medicine and psychoanalysis become fully beneficial only when they recognize liberation and development of the personal subject's true nature as their ultimate task. When research and treatment genuinely focus on the person, traditional medicine becomes even more useful—not least because the harmful body/soul dichotomy of rational thought is left behind. Personally seen, soul and body are not separate realities, but the two modes in which we express what we are inwardly and outwardly—that is, experience it inwardly, and manifest it outwardly.

The living body is not simply an animated corpse, but the mode in which we manifest, express, and realize ourselves as subjects in everything we do. Our ingrained or spontaneous ways of behaving can match our personal law or contradict it, can be open or closed to true nature, can be transparent or opaque. Doctors who see the personal subject in their patients do not focus merely on a sick part of the body, but on total bodily state, which reveals a person's subjective way of *being there*, and shows whether he or she is permeable to true nature or imprisoned in the ego. The patient's overall attitude, tension/relaxation balance, and breathing all indicate whether, and to what extent, he or she is confined in the fretful, angst-ridden ego, or properly centered, relaxed, and confident. "Wrong" posture, tension, or physical slackness, and above all shallow breathing tell doctors that a basic trust and serenity are lacking, and thus that true nature is being blocked. They counter this by teaching the patient to attain, through right posture, relaxation, and breathing, the bodily state that is permeable to true nature and can therefore release its deep-down healing energies. But just as doctors cannot deal adequately with their patients as personal subjects unless they obey their own personal law, so they cannot give the help that comes from right posture, relaxation, and breathing unless they take their own bodies seriously as the expression of their personhood, and constantly practice right posture themselves.

This is an area of which most modern doctors still know very little, and the blame for this lies with the excessively materialistic, rational views of the body that have so far prevailed. But doctors who move over to personal medicine, attending compassionately both to the anguish caused the world-ego by the world and to the anguish inflicted on true nature by that ego, are by no means obliged to leave their purely medical skills behind. Indeed, personal therapy in the broadest sense rests on three things: an objective approach to the medical problem, compassion for the suffering patient, and the strength to lead him or her on the way to personhood. In other words, the right kind of doctor has:

1. A sound knowledge of conventional medicine, which shows itself in an impartial, objective approach to the patient and in the keeping of a certain distance. On its own, however, this attitude turns patients into "cases" and ignores them as human beings;

2. A warm, sympathetic heart, and the ability to understand, empathize, and establish close contact with the patient. Even with this added quality, however, the doctor's help is still limited to the natural ego and the here-and-now body;

3. A deep-seated awareness and appreciation of the inner Way, which the personal law obliges human beings to follow. This allows the doctor to look beyond everything else to the patient's inner process of maturing and, on the basis of compassion and trust, restore the distance needed if he or she is to be truly summoned and guided on the way to personhood.

COMPASSION AND THE
PSYCHOTHERAPIST

The "personal approach" is adopted in psychotherapy, as it is in general medicine, when the patient stops being an object and becomes a "you," and when the therapist stops relating as specialist to "case," and starts relating person to person. This automatically brings compassion into play—but the need to maintain a certain distance is still there. This is a problematic area, and the problems are essentially due to the coexistence of two contradictory attitudes in the therapist—one that is cool, objective, and detached, and another that is warm, human, and intimate. The resultant inner conflict is accentuated for the therapist by the rival demands of science, which fears that personal contact will lead to mutual involvement and distort the judgment, and of the heart, whose feelings cannot be denied once the patient is seen as a fellow human being. Preserving an objective distance also becomes harder as the patient's sufferings start to affect the therapist, who feels an instinctive urge to trade professional detachment for human responsibility and help bear the burden. This conflict can become catastrophic, as it did in the case of Hans Trüb, who quarreled tragically with C. G. Jung on this very issue.

In his posthumous book *Heilung aus der Begegnung* (*Encounter Healing*, eds. Michel and Sborowitz, Stuttgart: Klett, 1951), Trüb takes his own career as a therapist and uses it to illustrate the limits of objectivity. The attitude he advocates depends on respect for the patient as person, and on the therapist's also committing himself or herself as person, and ultimately subordinating any scientific strategy for cure to the patient's personal reality and truth.

The requirement that the patient be treated as a person is often erroneously taken to mean that the therapist must not just be objectively scientific, but personally supportive as well. In reality, focusing on the person means a *total* attitude change, affecting both the way in which we see and think about others objectively, and the way in which we see and deal with them as fellow human beings.

Some time ago, Paul Christian gave a particularly penetrating account of the ambivalent situation created by the simultaneous presence in therapy of the two possible ways of relating to others. He made the following distinction between "meeting" and "encountering": "To meet another person is to interpret him or her in terms of the objectively coherent, explicable world. To encounter him or her as a person is something utterly different. Encountering another person is a matter of sharing directly in his or her existence, of identifying vitally, unreservedly with his or her actions, of personal commitment, and of mutual understanding and complicity."*

It is only superficially, however, that the problems of psychotherapy are those of a conflict between objective and compassionate approaches to the patient. The real conflict is

* "Antreffen und Begegnung" in *Jahrbuch für Psychologie und Psychotherapie*, Vol. 1/III, 1958.

between a natural attitude that conditions both the objective and the compassionate approach, and a "supernatural" attitude that transcends both of them. As long as we see the problem as the clash of "cool" and scientific with "warm" and compassionate, we are not focusing fully on the person, but are still operating within the prepersonal, "natural" ego's reference system, which reduces everything to an antithesis—objective and tangible versus subjective and inward.

This reference system also lies behind the discredited assumption that the scientific outlook, which triumphs in technical mastery of the world, also holds the key to understanding human beings and leading them in the right way. Equally untenable is the assumption that compassion stops us from seeing and knowing clearly because it operates in the contingent, here-and-now world of joy and sorrow, union, and separation (although it is, of course, subjective, and can thus interfere with objective knowing and lead to personal involvement). Both of these assumptions are prejudiced, and together reflect the worldview of those who are still confined to "natural" ways of seeing, and have yet to experience the possibility of genuine transcendence. This worldview must be overcome.

Indeed, our task today is to transcend the prepersonal vision of life. To do that, we must genuinely accept the familiar, but rarely fruitful, insight that the scientific notion of objective reality (admittedly valid for one limited aspect of medicine) is aberrant when applied to the human being as person. As Christian puts it, "The scientific vision of humanity is a kind of organised diminution of its personhood." We must also get rid of the idea that we can relate to people personally only by having an emotional stake in their lives. Strange as it sounds, Christian is totally right when he says that *personal* encounter "has nothing to do with the various ways in which an affective or emotional relationship can impinge on us," and also when he adds: "To this extent, even transference and countertransference in psychotherapy belong on the level of meeting, rather than encounter." Relating to other people personally by seeking them out on the way to the self is not primarily a matter of partnering them in the here-and-now world, but of *belonging supra-personally together in otherworldly Life*. It is this dimension, and the realization of impeded true nature, that first gives the relationship meaning—and that meaning carries into loyal, compassionate companionship in the midst of worldly suffering.

Once we start seeing people as persons, we can no longer look at them in the way that turns them into objects —physical or mental—or meet them as the faceless, neutral vehicles of biological, spiritual, intellectual, or social functions. Each of them now encounters us as a definite someone—a someone who wants to be seen, taken seriously, and responded to as a person, and to be liberated into a new life from his or her true nature. The meeting of world-egos (therapist and patient) gives way to personal encounter. And whatever the patient's problem may be, this existential relationship provides the only basis for seeing and treating it properly— always assuming that the therapist cares about the *Way*. Similarly, that problem's only significance, once the patient is seen as a person, is that of a pointer to progress on the Way.

Human beings can be seen as persons only with the personal eye, and its opening depends on a link with the absolute dimension, whose urge to self-manifestation is expressed in our own drive toward self-fulfillment, and unites us all as brothers and sisters in Being. This latter relationship is the only one that is truly personal, and it cancels the antithesis between objectively knowing and compassionately helping, revealing them as twin aspects of the same absolute connection. Knowing at this point means uniting, and it "opens" the person known—not only to the therapist or guide, but also to himself or herself. Like the whole of life, therapy differs fundamentally, depending on whether it is experienced by an ego that relies entirely on rational knowledge and is still entangled in its worldly concerns, or by the subject that transcends ego-vision and existence, and opens to itself in the Absolute.

The therapist can prevent the patient's inner truth from appearing either by adopting the cool, objective stance that prevents him or her from seeing properly, or by yielding to the "loving impulses" that result in emotional involvement. Both approaches show that the relationship is not anchored in the therapist's own suprapersonal depths, but is still entirely secular. Inevitably, it misses the patient's suprapersonal reality and deepest personal aspiration—to be released from the ego and break through to true nature.* True nature itself also stays hidden as long as the therapist focuses primarily on the patient's here-and-now body. In this situation, there is a danger that therapist and patient will check each other's progress, and that danger recedes only when the therapist stops operating mainly from the world-ego, and starts operating from true nature and focusing steadily from it on the patient's metaphysical center, and on realization of that center in his or her here-and-now body. It recedes even further when the real healing process begins—when true nature's individuality assumes here-and-now form, and so puts an end to the rule of the world-afflicted ego, which knows nothing of real freedom and merely oscillates between keeping a cold distance and becoming emotionally, clingingly involved.

The sterile tension between objective knowledge and personal involvement is thus resolved when progressive fusion with his or her own true nature takes the therapist so far beyond the determining ego, with its objective fixations and

* Cf. Dürckheim: "Das Überpersönliche in der Übertragung," in *Erlebnis und Wandlung* (Stuttgart/Berne: Huber, 1956).

universal entanglements, that the relationship with the "patient" can also take root in the other dimension.

Thinking in terms of personal therapy forces us to adjust our notions of "knowledge" and "involvement." "Knowledge" is no longer objective knowing, which generates rational concepts, but existential knowing, which connects with the known's true nature and frees it to itself. Similarly, "involvement" comes to mean a relationship that redeems and heals precisely because it brings true nature's truth to light—which it can do only if it has its own roots in personal true nature, and not in the contingent here and now, which either keeps us impersonal, cold, and detached, or threatens us with private, personal involvement. True nature also provides the only basis for elimination of the general obstacle inherent in domination of consciousness by the subject/object pattern. This type of consciousness makes transcendence impossible—although this, of course, matters little to the kind of therapy that aims solely at restoring lost function. Once something more than the skilled removal of ingrained complexes and fixed mechanisms is at issue, however, the consciousness ruled by the clinging, rational ego must be left behind—a necessary prelude to the therapy that is not content simply to help people who still know nothing of true nature to meet the world's demands, and restore their capacity for enjoyment, work, and love in a worldly sense. It is only when therapy is ruled by the spiritual principle that wakes when Being is experienced, is formed in the deep-down experience of inner law and pattern, and becomes responsible, governing consciousness, that the true compassion shines out—the compassion that has power both to heal and to illuminate. These two effects—illumination and healing—are combined when the therapist looks past the patient's physical problems to the form that his or her inner self is trying to assume. Here again, it is vital not to see that form outside here-and-now reality. It must be seen *in* here-and-now reality—as a disposition of the here-and-now body that accords with true nature, is transparent to it, and witnesses to it in the world. The true light reveals true nature *in* the here-and-now form to which the world-ego clings, and touches its core in a way that dissolves the body's resistance to inner form, freeing that form and allowing it to emerge creatively. This, in fact, is a light that both redeems and creates. It redeems by addressing the individual's true nature in such a way that he or she opens, "thaws," and responds—perhaps for the first time ever—from his or her true nature, discarding ready-made responses and all the accretions of habit. It creates by kindling his or her own inner light and triggering the process of creative change. When the frozen ground opens, the waiting seed flowers from the living depths beneath.

MATURITY AND OLD AGE

Most people naturally wish that they could stay young forever and never grow old. This is understandable enough but, once that wish becomes a fear of growing old, it has serious long-term consequences, since it robs us of the fulfillment that old age is meant to bring us. Compliance with Life's law is the only route to that fulfillment—and this includes acceptance of the aging process. That acceptance itself is only possible if our lives are rooted in a reality beyond the young/old antithesis, a reality that makes old age the ultimate test and example—joyously demonstrating the presence of the Absolute, which reveals itself in becoming *and* in ceasing to be. Of course, people who lack real contact with the Absolute are astonished at the thought that old age can bring fulfillment—for them it means a sad, painful decline toward an unavoidable end. They are totally unaware that the meaning of all the darknesses of life is always the light they conceal. In the darkness of old age, too, there is a meaning and, once it is disclosed, old age is no longer the dreaded final chapter, but life's true climax and celebration, for the first time bringing us that ultimate maturity on which our fulfillment depends. Human maturity is thus the meaning of life's final phase—and that meaning is missed by those who reject the aging process. But what are the real implications of all this?

The sufferings of old age are genuine, and only those who take them seriously have the right to speak of a dimension that points beyond them. The old face three dangers. The first is the loss of physical and mental capability—illness, invalidism, and at last, inevitably, death. The second is loss of meaning. How often we hear old people say, "My life has lost its meaning!"—simply because they are no longer able to "do" things, or make themselves useful! The third is the increasing loneliness that often comes with old age.

People who have led the initiatory life are largely immune to all this. They are affected only on the ego-surface of their personhood, and have more effective ways of warding off the things that nonetheless get through than others who are still reacting on a primitive level. The latter try desperately to conceal from themselves and from others the signs that they are growing old. They do everything possible to insure against *material want*. They normally attempt to prevent *loss of meaning* by making themselves useful in various minor ways and so proving to themselves and others that they still count for something—or rely on "intellectual distractions" to take their minds off growing old. When families fail to provide companionship, old people's clubs and retirement homes help to stave off loneliness. All of this is perfectly natural and—within certain limits—perfectly healthy as well. And yet it is a way of thinking that misses the real meaning of old age. People who are too careful in a material sense, who think that "doing" and "producing" are the purpose of life, and who are afraid of being alone, are basically running away from themselves. That is exactly what many old people are doing today—as the sun goes down, they are conscious only of the lengthening shadows. Only those who have followed the initiatory path are aware that a brighter star is coming into view on the horizon, rolling back the shadows and heralding a new day. They are also aware that fading and failing of the natural, external energies makes way for the supernatural, internal energies, and that human life is not fulfilled until those energies emerge. People who are in touch with the greater Life within know that it transcends our earthly life—and death. On the other hand, people who treat death as a specter, and run from reminders of it, plainly lack this contact. Most old people in this category are less the victims of old-age infirmities than of an anti-life attitude that rejects the aging process and resists the change proper to this stage.

The situation is totally different with old people who let things go calmly when their time has come, and give the new a trusting, open welcome, instead of clinging to the old. We all know very old people who have all the physical problems of age, but do not really suffer from them—who are content in spite of their infirmities and seem to treat death as an old friend, to whom they trust themselves gladly. This, however, is unusual. Far more common is the old person who has not achieved maturity and who oppresses a whole family, clings stubbornly to prerogatives, refuses to compromise, is demanding and tyrannical, poisons the atmosphere by perpetually finding fault with others, and is so self-involved that all offers of affection are simply brushed aside. People like this are so burdensome to others that everyone secretly longs for them to die—but they are also, and chiefly, a burden to themselves. Like all the painful vices of old age, their rigidity, bitterness, and self-absorption are signs that the maturity that age should bring has not been achieved. They have taken root in fixities and turned their back on further growth.

The only way to mature is to let go repeatedly, overcome the ego's attachments, listen to the inner voice, and unite with deeper meaning in unceasing change. Meister Eckhart's dictum "God's being is our becoming" means that God's nature is revealed to us only when we ourselves are continually on the way to becoming something else. Becoming is the key to living as we are meant to live—and witnessing in our own way to the Absolute, of which our true nature makes us part.

We can find life-fulfillment in the deepest sense only if we keep on growing and maturing to the end. Conversely, by pausing and clinging to fixities (particularly definite ideas concerning our life and its meaning), we close ourselves to the dimension that is trying to emerge, in and through us, from our innermost true nature to the light. Once our own inner longings have been stifled, anguish and dread take over, and we are left to end our days in bitterness and despair. But people who accept old age and are ready to keep changing till the end may well find that the failing of their natural powers allows supernatural powers to develop. If they only accept and let go, they may well feel that another, greater Life is calling them from within and, if they learn to hear its summons, filling them with something totally new. Once the soul leaves its worldly ties behind, otherworldly wealth and strength start to make their presence felt. This is a strength that supports and shields us, however frail and alone we may be. Old people who are given it may astonish us by developing a strange new radiance, and indeed changing visibly. Instead of growing hard, bitter, reserved, and a burden to themselves and others, they become increasingly relaxed, calm, cheerful, and good-natured. What does all of this mean? It means that they have outgrown their worldly nature—which naturally grieves at the ending of its little life—and transformed it from true nature, which now shows through clearly to their own and others' benefit. It is by witnessing in this way to the Absolute within us that old age fulfills itself in matured human form and bears its noblest fruit—fruit that now falls as naturally and effortlessly as a ripe apple from the tree. This fruit is the hidden working of the inner Way. All the worldly realities we can understand (and sometimes control) are simply a prelude to a deeper reality, of which we are no longer masters, but servants. If we serve it faithfully, however, it makes us the lords of this world by giving us powers that relieve our natural sufferings from a supernatural source.

When our natural strength is exhausted, and we humbly accept that fact, a supernatural strength takes over, making us aware of a higher Life that fills us, lifts us into another dimension, and enables us to face death calmly. This is why we should pattern ourselves not on those hearty oldsters who take a gleeful pride in showing us how active they still are, but on old people who accept their own weakness reverently and and so enter otherworldly order and strength, which their cheerful serenity then mirrors and incorporates. This serenity robs even death of its sting, and subdues the incomprehensible to a deeper meaning. It is only to those who look death in the face without flinching that higher Life already reveals itself in this one. This is also the secret of those old people who stay young in this deeper sense. They stay young because they are serenely ready, when their time comes, to surrender all their links with life and let them go. No longer clinging to anything, they become permeable to inner experience of the greater Life that rules us all and is now speaking from them. Lifted above time and everyday concerns, they face the future with confidence, secure in the promise of the new motive energy within them. Nostalgia, with its ceaseless, sentimental rehashing of the past, is left behind—and so is the secret dread of imminent death. There is a mysterious brightness in their eyes—a brightness that speaks of the eternal new beginning, beyond past and future, in which our whole existence is repeatedly remade and renewed by the Absolute.

The radiance of mature old age has nothing to do with

a person's natural powers, and the wisdom of old age has nothing to do with a lifetime's accumulated knowledge. Completely unconnected with possessions, knowledge, and abilities, this wisdom and strength are one of Being's modes—readiness to accept and freedom to let go. The wiser an old person is, the more calmly he or she accepts the failing of memory. Mature human wisdom is focused on something that can no longer be conceptualized, because it reaches into a dimension that cannot be understood. This is also why it is expressed less in words than in a profound, understanding, and benevolent silence.

Just as old age has a special strength and wisdom, so it also has a special, otherworldly, conciliatory, and forgiving kindness—a warmth that melts the frozen, straightens the crooked, and brings divided hearts together. This is a quality that witnesses to the presence of a higher dimension and tells us that all living things are fundamentally, profoundly connected—are one in true nature.

When old people understand what aging really means, the earlier stages in their lives are illuminated too. Above all, it becomes clear why certain actions have positive effects. Those effects have nothing to do with physical strength, technical skill, determination, or intelligence—and even "goodwill" is not enough. They are due to a link with the Absolute, experienced on the deepest level, which lives on as conscience, energizes the action, and lights it up from within, giving it meaning and value, and infusing it with love.

Whenever worldly life has remained whole or become whole again, it is permeable to otherworldly Life—and the same is true of human beings. Ultimately, this transparency to the Absolute is the goal of all spiritual development—and it increasingly becomes the real and only meaning of existence for old people who keep on maturing to the end. This is even truer when they succeed in shedding the notion that they still have a duty to "contribute." It actually becomes harder for them to live the real meaning of old age, and not simpler, when others conceal their disabilities from them, overlook their bad qualities, and try at all costs to preserve their illusion of continuing "usefulness." All of this is human enough, but it betrays a profound misunderstanding of life's real issues. The meaning and dignity of old age have nothing to do with overt worldly activity, but depend on transparency to a higher dimension, from which an inner light shines as otherworldly strength, wisdom, and kindness. The *fruit of human maturity is a beneficial light* that a person radiates without "doing" anything (or, better, that lies beyond activity and inactivity). The greater the maturity that people have won in living, working, and facing up to hardship, the easier they find it to see this —the real meaning of old age—as opportunity and as obligation. They not only can, but should, know that their final duty in this world is to bring redemption, meaning, and renewal from within—not by doing, but simply by existing.

Surely, people who ask about the meaning of life should simply be told: "The meaning of life is what is happening at the precise point in the universe where you are standing, walking, lying, or sitting at this moment—whatever you are doing or not doing. The only thing that matters is the kind of energy that goes out from that spot—whether it brings life or death, light or darkness, warmth or cold."

It is our aura—our personal atmosphere, mood, stillness, and radiance—that ultimately determines whether we fail in our supreme task or succeed in it and serve ourselves and others by reaching that state of maturity in which we become windows for the creative energy, ordering brightness, and redeeming warmth of the divine light that is our life's true center.

Just as it takes the sun to light up the colors of a stained-glass window and reveal the picture in them, so our deep-down true nature is revealed only when we become transparent to the inner light, from which we all live—and that banishes even death with its brightness.

PARTNERING THE DYING

How we die depends on how we live. There are countless ways of living, and so there are countless ways of dying. Our attitude toward death reflects our attitude toward life, and our dying shows what we understood by "living."

Believing that here-and-now life is the whole of the story makes suffering meaningless and reduces death to an enemy. People who think this way are afraid of dying. People who have learned to sense otherworldly Life through here-and-now living, however, see that worldly life is already a prelude to otherworldly Life, which infuses and transcends it, and thus a preparation for death. But absolute Life only opens in us fully when contingent life is allowed to end. This is true at all stages of our living, and is also the real meaning of our dying.

When one Christian partners another in the hour of death, and does this in a consciously Christian spirit, both know exactly what is expected of them. The things said, the help given, and the support provided are all rooted in the faith of the one, and accepted in the faith of the other. All of this also shows, of course, just how sincerely that faith is held.

But what happens when someone who has no "beliefs" is dying—someone who can no longer believe, or cannot yet believe? This situation instantly shows whether the helper is merely professing a belief, or has the real faith that comes of personal experience, commitment, and change. That faith is essential if he or she is to wake in the dying person the resounding tones of the reality that living was meant to reveal—and that dying must reveal now. This opens the way to a kind of spiritual care that is not just a matter for ministers or priests, but for any caring human being.

The only people who can fully accompany another person on his or her last journey are those who have themselves experienced the reality that bursts all the world-ego's boundaries, and they must have taken this experience seriously—and indeed accepted it as the source and meaning of their own attitude toward life.

We live in an age in which millions of people have been forced to look death in the face, and have come in this way to direct, personal experience of a reality beyond death and life. To most of them, this reality had been merely a pious belief until then—and experiencing it has brought them through. It is taking this kind of experience seriously that allows us to reach maturity. And only people who have this maturity can truly accompany a dying person into the infinity beyond death's dark door.

We reach full maturity only when our own experience makes otherworldly Life a vital presence for us, and we acknowledge it, unite with it, and are changed by it in a way that frees us of worldly ties. When we have this maturity, we *know* about the Life that both transcends death and depends on it. At this stage, death ceases to be an enemy and becomes a brother and companion—not just when we are actually dying but, if we live rightly, throughout our lives as well. Partnering the dying depends on seeing death in these terms.

For Western Christians, living and dying are both summed up in the cross. Unless they have *experienced* the other reality, however, the image of Christ on the cross remains terrible even for those who want to believe that resurrection is the meaning of death, for it shows them the very death that the natural ego dreads—terrifying, final, and followed by judgment and damnation. It is an image that makes fear of death completely natural, and this changes only when we have already sensed the reality of Life in life, have taken that experience seriously, and have hung onto it as knowledge and promise. This takes the fear out of dying, which simply becomes a matter of going home to a country one has never really left. An old missionary once explained to me that, for the Japanese, being born is like stretching one leg into the world, and keeping the leg that really bears our weight on the other shore—and so dying is simply a matter of drawing the extended one back to the place where we have secretly been all the time. It is not a question of *having* to die, but of *being allowed* to die. This explains the traditional practice of the old Zen masters who, when they sensed that their time had come, invited their students and friends to a last meal, at which the sacred tea ceremony was performed. Later, in the presence of their guests, they allowed themselves to sink into the great stillness, the deep, meditative calm they had practiced all their lives—death of the ego from which, this time, they simply failed to return. Consciously, smilingly, they entered otherworldly Life, knowing (and not merely believing) that they, deep down in their true nature, were—and had always been—that Life themselves.

Are these two visions—death as the world-ego's enemy and death as the friend of the inner self, which emerges when that ego collapses and fuses with true nature—really incompatible? Only for the static understanding! For the truth lies in the Way's eternal "dying and becoming." The Way, on which divine Being is revealed in our human process of dying and becoming, *is* Life, and also the truth of human existence. The Absolute's presence is not just something we believe in, but something we are allowed to experience, and are expected to witness to—witness, in other words, to the fact that the dying that the world-fixated ego finds so painful is essential to the opening of true nature, in which otherworldly Life is within us. Contact with the Absolute is both essential and sufficient to give us a serene acceptance of the here-and-now limits that death imposes on us. For people who have practiced this kind of dying all through their lives, death becomes a companion, and leads them over the threshold from life writ small into Life writ large. Practicing dying is central to all Life-directed exercise. This is age-old wisdom, but how often is it applied? The whole of life can be a rehearsal for dying—but this can be taught only when the spiritual teacher is himself filled with the promise of Life, and when Life is already present in the student as intuition and longing. Good intentions are not enough if we want to let the worldly ego die. We must also be in touch with our true nature, for only that can free us to let go. Releasing this freedom is the task of anyone who sets out to partner a dying person, and to do it he or she must already be in touch with the other dimension, know about the personal law of becoming from direct experience, and have tried to follow that law by becoming permeable for the Absolute. Dying provides a special opportunity to attain precisely this permeability, for dying means that the world-directed, world-entangled ego lets go—and, when it does, true nature may shine out.

A person who dies as an ego is still not a corpse, is still not really dead; for true nature may suddenly infuse the still responsive substance of the body at this very moment, giving the face the transparency known as the radiance of death. People who have no feeling for what is happening here take this simply for the "calm" that follows suffering. To those who can see, however, it is clear that otherworldly true nature is manifesting itself—radiant, pure, and in harmony with its own inner form. Only people who can see this are able to accompany others over the threshold.

People who see death as the enemy of life think in terms of having to die, and regard this as a misfortune. People who think in terms of being allowed to die have been given the promise of absolute Life, which includes the death of here-and-now life. As we have seen, there are three sources of suffering—annihilation, absurdity, and utter loneliness—in the here and now, and fear, despair, and grief are our natural reactions to them. When people who still identify completely with the world-ego are approaching death, they experience all three types of suffering more powerfully than ever before. But at this very moment, they may find—if they let go, if they accept dying—that a new light dawns in each: from helplessness, the experience of otherworldly strength; from meaninglessness, the sense of otherworldly order; and from utter solitude, the experience of otherworldly love. In other words, they experience dying as the start of a new life. All of this depends, of course, on giving up everything they cling to, for only then is the way clear for the other dimension to enter, for transparency to become operative and beneficial.

In this sense, the whole of life should be a preparation for transparency, a preparation for dying in the right way—just as dying in the right way signals the quality of the life that led up to it.

Dying may show us another reality, of which natural ways of thinking and seeing can give us at best a pale reflection—and those ways of thinking and seeing may yield to a new consciousness precisely when we are dying. Dying offers us, as it were, an opportunity to give up our partial way of seeing and let a ray from the Whole enter and illuminate our inner nature. The right companion's presence can help to bring us revelation of the Whole by leading us toward that new and broader consciousness. Simply by being there, he or she can enable us to release our grip on ego-world consciousness. Death approaches gently and loosens the chains with which ego-consciousness (which has so far stopped us from admitting otherworldly Life and taking it seriously) binds us to the world, while that consciousness fades out. Of course, the right kind of companion also knows that otherworldly consciousness can emerge only in counterpoint to the worldly consciousness that blocks it.

When we are dying, the ego reasserts itself powerfully, summoning up all our natural energies to maintain its hold on life. Often enough, this happens even when the person concerned is perfectly ready to die—death is a struggle for everyone. Particularly when the resistance is strong, however, Life may be revealed in a special way when the ego collapses. It is not until we actually reach the dividing line that we are ready for whatever lies beyond it. It is precisely in the pitlike final darkness that the mighty light of a new beginning may shine out, and precisely when the finite draws to an agonizing close that the infinite may make itself felt. Anyone who partners and comforts a dying person must know that it is not enough to put the world behind one, reject the darkness, admit and regret one's mistakes, or even turn solely to the light, when death approaches. At this stage, it is more important to release the creative, transforming energies of the darkness, which burst out when the darkness itself is fully recognized and accepted.

For us, death really means the end. All the things we have built come tumbling down. All our rational insights turn worthless. All our facades and pretenses cave in, revealing the often pathetic reality of what we actually were. As the things we had, knew, and relied on fail us, we are thrown back on ourselves, and at the same time find ourselves at the mercy of a greater, incomprehensible, and unknown power. In our helplessness, we naturally fear annihilation. All the lies that we spun about our life evaporate. Our own guilt comes crushingly home to us, and we suddenly know that everything is wrong. To all this is added the sorrow of loneliness, for we are never more alone than when we are dying. In this situation, what could be more natural than to look for comfort or compassion from someone close to us? But compassion itself can be a serious threat if the loyal companion makes the mistake of offering sympathy, comfort, false hope, and nothing more; for this is one sure way of robbing the dying of the fruit not just of suffering but of the whole of life as well.

There are times when comfort is an injustice, indeed a crime against the healing spirit—times when it enables people who are dying, and might otherwise have changed, to stay the way they are, or interferes at the very moment when the purifying fires of hopeless despair and impenetrable loneliness are on the point of melting and remolding them.

It is only when we accept and endure the unendurable, release the things we cannot bear to let go—in short when we accept death of the old Adam, who must die before we die ourselves—that death's nearness can bring life to final fruition, for we are closest to the other dimension when we actually reach the crossing point. When we come to it, we need a friend and partner who also has the strength to leave us alone. No attempt must be made to take the experience of utter helplessness from us, for this prevents us from making the ultimate decision. At the right moment, we must be left to ourselves, so that, as the ego's lonely dying transforms us, we can experience for ourselves the light that is the meaning of all darkness, and the love that is the meaning of all loneliness.

Partnering the dying is a task that anyone may have to

undertake. In practice, it rarely falls to priests or ministers, although caring for souls is their profession. But for them, too, traditional pastoral ways of helping the dying are not enough—they also need human fellow-feeling, and a sense of "brotherhood in Being." There are, in fact, three approaches:

1. The first is the "classical" deathbed approach of the priest or minister, who looks beyond the dying person's particular circumstances and personal anguish and attempts to lift him or her through faith out of general human misery into the lofty realms of divine promise. Like tried and true remedies, traditional words are spoken, venerable formulas recited, comforting axioms repeated, and prayers recommended—and all of this is done in impersonal reliance on the power of God and redemption by Christ, and in no way depends for its effectiveness on the pastor's personal involvement. Only an out-and-out rationalist would scorn and dismiss the precious power of faith that is embodied, communicated, and manifested in supra-personal words, even—or particularly—when priests discharge their function in a wholly impersonal manner.

2. Next comes the personal approach of those spiritual guides who see the dying as fellow human beings who are suffering in the world-ego and are afraid to die. To relieve this anguish, they offer compassion and support, helping the dying to open up and shed their burdens by speaking out trustingly and frankly, admitting their anxieties and revealing their longings. In this way—and perhaps by speaking of their own anguish and their own guilt—these helpers enable them to shake off the many chains with which the "proud" world-ego binds them to the last, and to shed the illusion of still being able to cross the threshold "with dignity." In this way, they help them to find inner truth, to let all the facades come

down, and to open themselves in their full naked helplessness to the great unknown that is drawing inexorably nearer.

3. Finally, there are those who approach the dying from true nature to true nature, as brothers and sisters in Being. There can be no question here of staying on the level of compassionate feeling and shared human suffering, or of transcending personal anguish and witnessing impersonally to the promise of faith. What counts here is to look believingly, lovingly, and yet unsparingly into the dying person's true nature, summon him or her on the self's deepest level, call him or her—silently perhaps—into the truth, and give him or her the strength to bear the painful flickering out of the ego that agonizes at having to let go. All of this so that, when worldly life draws to its pathetic close, otherworldly Life can blaze out untainted. Assisting at this slow extinction of the ego makes supreme demands on the deathbed partner who is, paradoxically, acting as midwife at a kind of birth—and neither the birth itself nor the pain that goes with it can be spared the dying person. The partner can only help to create the conditions in which purified physical existence can finally come to fruition. The love this requires is a higher, suprapersonal love, and it depends, however hard this may be, on overcoming the other, merely compassionate love, the love that binds wounds, soothes anxiety, dries tears, and tells lies out of kindness—all to protect the dying person from the "painful" truth (as if fear of the truth were not always more terrible than the truth itself). Surely, indeed, the dying have a right to the truth? This raises the old question: how much truth should a dying person be told?

There is no easy answer to this, and everything depends on the extent to which we still respect a dying person's personal freedom—the freedom that makes us all responsible for living (and so dying) in the right way, and gives us all a right to the truth. Of course, the answer also depends on the maturity both of the partner and the dying person—and on the partner's realizing that death allows the dying person to become fully human for the last (and perhaps first) time. Dying is the final—and possibly greatest—test of our freedom.* We may hold out defiantly and try yet again to come through, or surrender freely, trustingly, and totally to a higher power. We may cling to our old way of seeing, our natural rights, and our skepticism—or we may intuit grace and higher meaning and open ourselves utterly to a light that we feel without knowing what it means. We can refuse to accept what is happening and shut ourselves off from it, or we can use our last spark of freedom to give ourselves consciously to the infinite love that is swelling powerfully within us. This is a deep and mysterious process, and over it there shines the cold star of truth—merciless, challenging, and yet filled with promise. It is this very truth that we may now experience, not simply as an obligation that we free ourselves by meeting, but as the promise of being redeemed from existence and carried into Life. Of course, the knowledge that we are dying revives the life-obsessed ego and makes it fight back—and this is where our partner must intervene and allow the voice of truth to ring out. For however we feel about dying, we sense the need for utter truthfulness only to the extent that we admit that this is what is happening to us. Does anyone have the right, when we are dying, to prevent us from experiencing the final challenge, and meeting it? This, more than ever before, is our unique opportunity to commit ourselves utterly and freely, allow all the masks to fall away, confess hidden faults, and forgive the faults of others. For approaching death tears all the barriers down, and it also opens the door to all-

* Cf. L. Boros: *Mysterium Mortis* (Olten/Freiburg: Walter, 1962).

resolving love, which can now break in when it is least expected.

Priests and ministers know from experience that the nearness of death can give the dying an unexpected freedom, and that hearing the truth can—perhaps after an instant of natural shock—allow otherworldly Life to stream in. They know how infinitely grateful the dying often are when a simple word at last allows them to back off from the game of mutual pretense that is often played out around a deathbed. In a matter of days, and often minutes, they develop and mature—change and are perfected—in a way that shows that life has been rightly lived to its end.

I shall never forget an experience of this kind that I once had myself. A friend was dying after a serious operation. His doctors knew this well enough, but had promised to send him home a week later to prepare for a second operation, which was to complete the cure. This was what I heard from his family when I met them at the hospital. When I entered his room, one look told me that he was dying. I asked his wife to leave me alone with him. He started talking about a lecture he was due to give a fortnight later, saying that he hoped to be well enough to deliver it himself, or at least dictate it for someone else to read. Behind everything he said, I had a clear sense that he actually knew that none of this was true. I took my courage in both hands and said, "My dear old friend, instead of thinking about your lecture, I think you should put it all behind you, and start thinking about the point that lies beyond life and death. Yes"—I repeated—"beyond life and *death*." The effect was electrifying. He closed his eyes. New life came into his face. Its ashen color was replaced by a rosy glow. A kind of light seemed to shine from it. Then he opened his eyes and, with an expression of infinite peace on his face, gave me his hand and said simply: "Thank you." Then he closed his eyes again, and I left. I told his wife that he only had a few days left. Here was a man who was not afraid of dying, and had the maturity to prepare for it consciously and calmly—and his dying was being spoiled for him. The nearer it came, and the more his need grew for utter peace—peace to be quietly with the woman who had shared his life, and peace, peace, peace for himself—the more the nurses came crowding round his bed with equipment and instruments to prolong his merely physical life for a few extra hours. At the very end, he was being deprived of the last thing he could still call his own—his death.

Why, when their time has come, are people not allowed to die in peace?

WORKS CITED

BOROS, L. *Mysterium Mortis* [The Mystery of Death]. Olten/Freiburg: Walter, 1962.

CUTAT, A. *La rencontre des religions* [The Meeting of Religions]. Paris: Aubier, 1957.

DÜRCKHEIM, KARLFRIED GRAF. "Die Bedeutung des Leibes in der Psychotherapie" [The Meaning of the Body in Psychotherapy] in Zacharias, *Festschrift für W. Bitter*. Stuttgart: Klett, 1968.

——. *Erlebnis und Wandlung* [Experience and Transformation]. Stuttgart/Berne: Huber, 1956.

——. *The Grace of Zen: Zen Texts for Meditation* (with others). New York: Seabury Press, 1976.

——. *Hara: The Vital Centre of Man*. Translated by Sylvia-Monica von Kospoth and Estelle Healey. London: Unwin Paperbacks, 1977.

——. "The Healing Power of Pure Gesture" in *The Way of Transformation: Daily Life as a Spiritual Exercise*. Translated by Ruth Lewinnek and P. L. Travers. London: Unwin Paperbacks, 1980.

——. "Mächtigkeit, Rang und Stufe des Menschen" [Human Power, Status and Maturity] in *Durchbruch zum Wesen*. Stuttgart/Berne: Huber, 4th edition, 1967.

——. *Sportliche Leistung—Menschliche Reife* [Sport, Performance and Maturity]. Munich: Limpert, 2nd edition, 1967.

————. "Wann ist der Mensch in seiner Mitte?" [When Are We Centered?] in Tenzler, *Die Wirklichkeit der Mitte - Festschrift für A. Vetter*. Munich: Alber, 1963.

————. *Im Zeichen der Grossen Erfahrung* [The Great Experience]. Weilheim/Obb.: O. W. Barth, 2nd edition, 1958.

————. *Zen and Us*. Translated by Vincent Nash. New York: E. P. Dutton, 1987.

ENOMIYA-LASSALLE, HUGO MAKIBI. *Zen-Buddhismus*. Cologne: J. P. Bachem, 1966.

————. *Zen: Way to Enlightenment*. New York: Taplinger Publishing Co., 1968.

EVOLA, JULIUS. "Über das Iniatische" [The Initiatory], in *Antaios*, Vol. V, No. 4.

GEBSER, JEAN. *The Ever-Present Origin*. Athens: Ohio University Press, 1985.

————. "Vermutungen über das unerschaffene Licht" [Speculations on the Uncreated Light], in M. Hippius (ed.) *Transzendenz als Erfahrung*. Weilheim/Obb.: O. W. Barth, 1967.

GOVINDA, LAMA ANAGARIKA. *Grundlagen tibetischer Mystik* [Fundamentals of Tibetan Mysticism]. Weilheim/Obb.: O. W. Barth, 3rd edition, 1972.

GUÉNON, RENÉ. *Aperçus sur l'initiation* [Initiation]. Paris: Les éditions traditionnelles, 1953.

————. *Le symbolisme de la Croix* [Symbolism of the Cross]. Paris: Les éditions Vega, 1957.

HERRIGEL, EUGEN. *Zen in the Art of Archery*. New York: Random House, 1971.

HIPPIUS, MARIA. "Beitrag aus der Werkstatt" [Contribution from the Workshop] in M. Hippius (ed.) *Transzendenz als Erfahrung*. Weilheim/Obb.: O. W. Barth, 1966.

JACOBS, HANS. *Indische Weisheit, westliche Therapie* [Indian Wisdom, Western Therapy]. Munich: Lehmann, 1966.

KÜKELHAUS, H. *Werkstatt, Forum 8*, 1967.

LOTZ, J. B. *Meditation im Alltag* [Everyday Meditation]. Frankfurt/M.: Knecht, 1966.

MÜLLER-ECKHARD, H. *Von der Krankheit, nicht krank sein zu können* [The Disease of Not Being Able to be Ill]. Stuttgart: Klett.

OTTO, RUDOLF. *Das Heilige*. Munich: Beck, 1987.

PELTZER, R. "Die Arbeit an der Transparenz über den Leib" [Working on Transparency through the Body], in M. Hippius (ed.) *Transzendenz als Erfahrung.*

TRÜB, H. *Heilung aus der Begegnung* [Encounter Healing], eds. Michel and Sborowitz. Stuttgart: Klett, 1951.

YASUTANI, HAKUIN. "Za-Zen" in Dürckheim (ed.). "Wunderbare Katze und andere Zen-Text." Weilheim/Obb.: O. W. Barth, 1975.

FOR THE BEST IN PAPERBACKS, LOOK FOR THE

In every corner of the world, on every subject under the sun, Penguin represents quality and variety—the very best in publishing today.

For complete information about books available from Penguin—including Pelicans, Puffins, Peregrines, and Penguin Classics—and how to order them, write to us at the appropriate address below. Please note that for copyright reasons the selection of books varies from country to country.

In the United Kingdom: For a complete list of books available from Penguin in the U.K., please write to *Dept E.P., Penguin Books Ltd, Harmondsworth, Middlesex, UB7 0DA.*

In the United States: For a complete list of books available from Penguin in the U.S., please write to *Dept BA, Penguin*, Box 120, Bergenfield, New Jersey 07621-0120.

In Canada: For a complete list of books available from Penguin in Canada, please write to *Penguin Books Canada Ltd, 10 Alcorn Avenue, Suite 300, Toronto, Ontario, Canada M4V 3B2.*

In Australia: For a complete list of books available from Penguin in Australia, please write to the *Marketing Department, Penguin Books Ltd, P.O. Box 257, Ringwood, Victoria 3134.*

In New Zealand: For a complete list of books available from Penguin in New Zealand, please write to the *Marketing Department, Penguin Books (NZ) Ltd, Private Bag, Takapuna, Auckland 9.*

In India: For a complete list of books available from Penguin, please write to *Penguin Overseas Ltd, 706 Eros Apartments, 56 Nehru Place, New Delhi, 110019.*

In Holland: For a complete list of books available from Penguin in Holland, please write to *Penguin Books Nederland B.V., Postbus 195, NL-1380AD Weesp, Netherlands.*

In Germany: For a complete list of books available from Penguin, please write to *Penguin Books Ltd, Friedrichstrasse 10-12, D-6000 Frankfurt Main 1, Federal Republic of Germany.*

In Spain: For a complete list of books available from Penguin in Spain, please write to *Longman, Penguin España, Calle San Nicolas 15, E-28013 Madrid, Spain.*

In Japan: For a complete list of books available from Penguin in Japan, please write to *Longman Penguin Japan Co Ltd, Yamaguchi Building, 2-12-9 Kanda Jimbocho, Chiyoda-Ku, Tokyo 101, Japan.*